The Pied Pipers of Autism

How Television, Video and Toys in Infancy Cause ASD

LEONARD OESTREICHER M.D.

The Author and his nephew, Otto

RESEARCH ASSISTANT
MARCIN OSSOWSKI

ILLUSTRATIONS AND GRAPHICS
ROBERT GARCIA AND ADAM OSSOWSKI

Comments from Readers----

In The Pied Pipers of Autism, Dr. Leonard Oestreicher addresses an important area that has long been overlooked by autism researchers. The world in which our children learn has changed significantly in the way that technology invades their early childhood, possibly distracting and robbing these children of critical early human experiences. Despite a possible link between television and autism suggested by Michael Waldman and Associates in 2006, no serious investigation into this area has been performed. Since the early 1990's, there has been a dramatic increase in availability and access to children's videos and cable television viewing options which previously did not exist, allowing extended early childhood viewing of media and viewing the same material frequently. The timing of this increased exposure to audiovisual media coincides with the increase in autism rates. While the American Academy of Pediatrics recommends no viewing by children younger than age two, many parents are not getting this message. Dr. Oestreicher, compelled by his desire to help decrease autism rates, delivers a compassionate and cohesive theory that will hopefully get the attention of parents and caretakers of infants and young children, pediatricians who advise and instruct in that care, and those involved with autism research.

Karen F. Heffler, MD

I believe you are onto something crucial. It's as though professionals (and the public) are afraid to see the obvious connection -- society becomes more oriented towards electronics -- and kids are chained to them from earlier and earlier age -- while autism rises -- and we continue to look under the rug for the boogeyman who causes the problem.

Stanton Peele PhD

Dr. Oestreicher has written an important book concerning the possibility that early childhood television watching is an important trigger for autism. Hopefully, the book will spur the autism medical community to pay attention to this plausible but long neglected hypothesis."

Michael Waldman PhD

The Pied Pipers of Autism
How Television, Video and Toys in Infancy Cause ASD
By Leonard Oestreicher MD
Copyright Leonard Oestreicher 2012

Please feel free to share this book with anyone who might be having a baby soon or has an interest in ASD. Thank you.

Preface

I admit the idea for this book came from my wife. She would discuss with me the odd behavior of her sister's son, Otto. She noticed he did not make eye contact, enjoy being held or playing with her. My wife told me when Otto was an infant he had watched and enjoyed the *Baby Einstein* video series. She thought he had enjoyed them too much.

Having raised my older children before the era of infant videos, I was unfamiliar with the idea of infant video education/entertainment. I thought the idea odd. When my wife's nephew was 3 years old, he started in daycare. He was plainly different from the other children and after a meandering and difficult path with all kinds of professionals; he was finally diagnosed with Autism Spectrum Disorder (ASD). ASD is a condition that disrupts the formation of social relationships and in the end socially isolates the child, even from his own family.

We were thinking about starting a family together at the time. Was the cause of ASD 90% genetic, as I had read, or something else? I had heard ASD was becoming a lot more common. Was there a connection between his enjoyment of the infant videos and his later development of Autism Spectrum Disorder (ASD)? It seemed to me the increased incidence of ASD and the increased exposure of infants to videos had occurred during the same period of time and on that basis was suspect.

I thought genetics alone could not explain the increasing incidence of this problem. It had to be something in the environment of these infants as well. Vaccines and the mercury in vaccines always seemed to me as very remote possible explanations. As a family physician, I understood the good these vaccines do in preventing fatal illnesses that were common during the time of my childhood. Subsequently, these explanations would be thoroughly discredited.

I started to talk to other people about my theory of autism. I looked on the internet for mention of the connection of video screen exposure to autism and found almost nothing. I tried to establish communication with experts in the field, who might be able to steer me to someone who was exploring this idea and got nowhere.

Then while listening to a course from the 'Teaching Company' about the nature of consciousness, I had a moment of insight. Almost all people assume other people have thoughts and awareness just like themselves, but it is impossible to prove. Everyone else could be zombies (objects that act and look like humans). How do you know for sure?

It struck me this is how people with autism must see the world. People must appear as objects. I realized once someone started to see people as being mere objects, it might be impossible to dispel this view. I wondered if infants' videos could encourage some babies to confuse people with objects. Could the toys and things babies see on TV and video be so compelling some babies lose interest in social relationships? Could this be why so many children today are developing ASD? These were my thoughts.

With that bit of insight, I started to feel guilty. If I was correct and infants' videos and the like were part of the cause of ASD, then I had a responsibility to share this idea as quickly and as convincingly as possible. Perhaps a lot of children could be prevented from ever getting ASD. But I was too involved with caring for my patients, my business interests, and a newborn child. I shared my guilty feelings with my wife again and again. I kept looking on the internet for someone else to make this connection. No one did. My wife finally said, why don't you just write a book about this idea if you feel so strongly about it.

When she said that, I realized I had to write this book. I have been a family physician, a software developer, and a real estate developer but I have never written a book. I ask my readers to forgive me if my writing is ever less than clear. I feel a great pressure to get this idea out to parents who are having children.

As I started to write the book with this idea in mind, I realized I was making a lot of statements that may or may not be supported by current academic literature. I had the amazing good fortune of finding my best friend's son not only semi-unemployed but already very informed on this very topic, having graduated from UCLA recently with a major in neurolinguistics.

I asked if he could help me do some research on this little book I was thinking about writing. He agreed and found literally hundreds of pertinent papers we diligently reviewed together. This exercise greatly deepened my understanding of ASD and my respect for all the brilliant minds who have been and who are researching this condition.

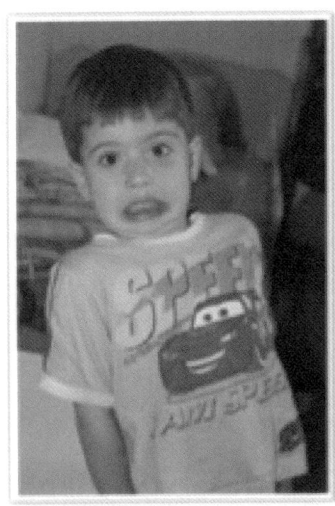

After reviewing the literature in much more detail, I realize I am merely connecting the dots, being the one who says 2 + 2 equals 4. All the chapters in this book deserve to be books by themselves. I have tried to make the immense literature about ASD accessible and understandable.

My hope, in the end, is my readers will protect their infants and toddlers from the spell of the Pied Pipers of Autism: Pied Pipers who can enrapture their children and take them away from the love and safety of their families.

- Leonard Oestreicher, MD

Friend Us at Facebook – Pied Pipers of Autism

Blog with Author at "toystvautism.com"

Thank you for sharing Your Thoughts...

Via One-Way Communications
Oliver Sacks, MD
Simon Baron-Cohen, FBA
Virginia Campbell MD & The Brain Science Podcast

Via Two-Way Communications
My Brother Donald Oestreicher, PhD

Dedication

To my wife Roseli,

Her sister Rosangela,

And Otto.

Once more he stept into the street,
And to his lips again
Laid his long pipe of smooth straight cane;
And ere blew three notes (such sweet
Soft notes as yet musician's cunning
Never gave the enraptured air)
There was a rustling
that seemed like a bustling
Of merry crowds justling at pitching and hustling,
Small feet were pattering, wooden shoes clattering,
Little hands clapping and little tongues chattering,
And, like fowls in a farm-yard when barley is scattering,
Out came the children running.
All the little boys and girls,
With rosy cheeks and flaxen curls,
And sparkling eyes and teeth like pearls,
Tripping and skipping, ran merrily after
The wonderful music with shouting and laughter.

Excepted from "Pied Piper of Hamelin" by Robert Browning

Table of Contents

PREFACE 4

INTRODUCTION 9

ABOUT OTTO- ONE ROSELI'S STORY 20

CHAPTER ONE SOCIAL NETWORKS 22

ABOUT OTTO – TWO ROSELI'S STORY CONTINUED 30

CHAPTER TWO THE SPECTRUM OF AUTISM SPECTRUM DISORDERS 31

ABOUT OTTO – THREE THE END OF ROSELI'S STORY 40

CHAPTER THREE THE BRAIN, LEARNING, AND ASD 41

ABOUT OTTO – FOUR ROSANGELA'S STORIES- ONE 53

CHAPTER FOUR GENDER 54

ABOUT OTTO – FIVE ROSANGELA'S STORIES- TWO 60

CHAPTER FIVE GENETICS 61

ABOUT OTTO – SIX ROSANGELA'S STORIES- THREE 77

CHAPTER SIX SOCIAL ENVIRONMENT 78

CHAPTER SEVEN TELEVISION, VIDEO AND TOYS 87

CHAPTER EIGHT TREATMENT 101

ABOUT OTTO – SEVEN 112

ROSANGELA'S STORIES- FOUR 112

CHAPTER NINE PREVENTION AND NEW DIRECTIONS .. 114

ABOUT OTTO- ROSANGELA'S STORY CONCLUSION 120

CONCLUSION OPPOSITION & REACTIONS 121

ABOUT THE AUTHOR 125

GLOSSARY 127

BIBLIOGRAPHY 140

Introduction

Autism.

What is going on?

On March 30, 2012 the CDC reported a staggering 23% increase between just 2006 and 2008 in the number of children being diagnosed with this frightening condition. Including the years from 2002 to 2008 there has been a 78% increase almost doubling the number of children with this calamitous disorder. Already 100,000s of children suffer with autism. And the numbers continue to climb. Something very wrong is going on here.

Parents, friends, teachers, family members want to know- why? There are two sides to the great debate about the cause of autism.

On one side, professors and academics maintain these increases are some sort of mass illusion, an urban legend, something that can't possibly be happening. They are lost in their genetic models of autism, each new model becoming more and more farfetched. All the while they continue to deny this great explosion in the number of children with ASD (Autism Spectrum Disorder).

On the other side, are the people searching for something in the environment to explain this pandemic as it spreads around the world. They believe vaccines, mercury, soaps, nano-chemicals, something in the rain or other even more bizarre and unlikely substances are the causes of ASD.

Both sides agree on one thing, the mysterious nature of autism. By mysterious, they mean the public will need to continue to fund research costing hundreds of millions of dollars for years and years to come. Meanwhile, the cost of caring for children with ASD continues to skyrocket, now estimated by the CDC to be an almost unbelievable 35 billion dollars a year.

I beg to differ from both sides in this great debate.

I believe the cause of autism and autism spectrum disorder is both simple and straight-forward. It is something anyone can understand and do something about today. It is something the American Academy of Pediatrics has warned about for years.

I believe the cause of this outbreak of Autism is a group of toxins.

These toxins are found in almost every house in this country but a mere 50 years ago hardly existed.

They are easily removed but today we are everyday more and more surrounded by their presence.

The toxins are not swallowed, breathed, or touched but enter the brain directly through the eyes and ears of susceptible babies and infants.

The toxins are the Pied Pipers of Autism; TV, videos, video devices and talking toys and they work their awesome damage by flooding out and replacing the social life of our babies and infants with one-way communication.

The story of ASD, how these toxins cause ASD, what can be done to stop this epidemic of autism today, and how to take care of children already damaged is the subject of this book.

The story starts with a brief look at the very social world we are born into.

Social Networks

We live our lives totally immersed in and surrounded by a sea of social communication. We are built to communicate using both our bodies and our brains. Like many other mammals, we have an innate ability to express and understand facial expressions and body language. But it is our ability to use language that sets our social communication skills apart from all other animals.

We are social animals who form and live in social networks that are truly larger than ourselves. Shared thoughts, ideas, and beliefs enable us to coordinate activities in a way impossible for other creatures.

But we are not the only social species by any means. All social species must by definition communicate. Many species, including bees, parrots, and our closest relatives, non-human primates, all face the same challenges of communication in a social network. All social species live together in groups in semi-permanent locations with the future of the each of member linked to the future of the group.

Even solitary species must communicate for behaviors which require coordinated action, such as courtship or caring for their young. It is in these instances of shared communication that we, as humans, can find animal behavior we really identify and empathize with.

Advances in communication have led the way for human progress. One can only imagine how each step, starting with body language and facial expressions, on to spoken, written, and then printed language; and in recent years to the internet, has enabled thoughts, ideas, and beliefs to be shared ever-increasingly widely and easily.

Humans, as social beings, need social networks to survive, and most likely have so since the beginning of our development as a species. As babies and infants, we are hopelessly dependent on our parents to act as our caregivers. There is a vital period of learning for the infant to develop the desire and the ability to communicate with the people around him. This channel of communication established in early infancy serves as the gateway for the toddler and older child to learn the language, ideas, behaviors and rules of the social networks he will be a part of.

Not every child develops this channel of communication that will tie them to their friends and family. Those who do not will instead develop a condition which has become significantly more prevalent in our modern era: Autism Spectrum Disorder (ASD).

Social Communication versus Self-Communication

Thinking One Thing and Saying Something Else

Humans have two basic forms of communication. The first is our consciousness or interior monologue, which I will refer to as *self-communication*. This is comprised of our private thoughts and mental existence only we know. No one can look into our minds (as of yet, thank goodness) and see or monitor what we are actually thinking or what we say to ourselves. In fact, humans are very adept at concealing this self-communication. We readily communicate in ways that hide our actual conscious thoughts or feelings. We easily say one thing while we are thinking something else. We are not always trustworthy.

Nevertheless, this inner stream of consciousness shares much of the same language we use for the second form of communication: *social communication*. Social communication is fundamentally a two-way operation with mutual feedback. For example, I express something to you. You hear, see, smell and maybe even touch me and react to those stimuli and express something back to me. And back and forth it goes. This is a *conversation* or an *interaction*. You pay attention to me and I pay attention to you.

There may even be eye contact. By your communication with me and our history together, I know I am important to you, worth paying attention to, and vice versa. Trust follows. It is this kind of interaction that forms the basis for *social communication* and enables the formation of social networks.

Without this exchange, other people are fundamentally unknowable and trust cannot develop. It is this conversational interaction that I am calling *social communication*. Mutual attention is the currency that binds our social relationships and networks together and gives life meaning.

Each of us has a genetic tendency to prefer some blend of social and self-communication. How much do we like or need having the attention of other people? Are we happier when we are around other people? Or are we happier being by ourselves with our own thoughts? Or do we like to go back and forth? There is a natural spectrum, undoubtedly connected to our genetic makeup, of people with different mixtures of these tendencies.

My first memory as a small child was sitting alone in my living room playing with something or other. I remember having a conversation with myself and thinking how much more interesting I found my own company to that of other kids and most adults. Based on that, you can infer where I lay on this spectrum. In fact, adolescence and early adulthood were real struggles for me to gain a decent level of social communication skills. Only in medical school, where I was forced to actually talk to strangers every day, did I finally develop a facility for social communication.

If social communication is so important to human existence (and it certainly is), then why do some people genetically prefer self-communication? In the context of evolution, how can it make sense? Here is one possible explanation, one guess really, I like.

Human social networks and cultures compete. They compete for resources, prestige, power and people. People who prefer self-communication devote more of their mental capacity to thinking alone and less to socializing. They are not as influenced by their social networks in their thoughts and are freer to explore ideas not yet present in their culture. Being so they often develop new, different, and at times better ideas.

If they can communicate these new ideas and thoughts, it can give their social networks and culture an advantage when competing with others. Cultures that accepted the idea creative people have special value had an advantage despite the fact these same people could be difficult to live and work with.

My explanation is a bit farfetched; nevertheless the biography section in libraries is full of stories that demonstrate this very fact. Many famous and creative people probably lay somewhere on the spectrum of Autism Spectrum Disorder. Every now and then you come across a genius like Benjamin Franklin, who was both an original thinker and a great social communicator but many original thinkers in history seem to have had some features of ASD.

One-Way Communication

This book is really a form of one-way communication from me, the author, to you, the reader. As I am writing, I am hoping this book will

Listening, Reading, Watching a Video

Forms of One-way Communication

express my ideas well enough that you may understand my thoughts. But I have no way of knowing what you are thinking, or even if you have a living existence, until you express something back to me. Until we establish two-way communication, to me, you are just a figment of my imagination.

We can never learn how to communicate socially from one-way communication. It can tickle our consciousness, make us aware of other people's ideas, thoughts, and emotions, or entertain us, but it cannot teach us how to communicate with other people. The learning of two-way communication must employ back and forth conversations or interactions with another living being. It cannot be simulated by toys, videos, or computers. It is a demanding skill taking place very rapidly in real time and on multiple levels at once.

The critical time to learn this form of communication is during infancy. Our teachers are the people around us, mostly our caregivers. If we miss this period for learning social communication, it is difficult to acquire later.

Joint Attention

The fundamental way infants learn social communication is through *joint attention*. I cannot emphasize enough how important *joint attention* is for the normal development of social communication in infancy. But what makes joint attention so important?

There are three ingredients to joint attention: the baby, the caregiver, and an object or an event the baby and caregiver can both see. The baby sees something and then turns its eyes to the eyes of the caregiver and then back again to the object or event in question. The first time this happens is a magical moment for the baby and the attentive caregiver.

The baby sees something. He looks to his caregiver and by looking at where his caregiver's eyes are directed, the baby can tell they are both looking the same thing. The caregiver does the very same thing when they look at the baby's eyes. They both know they are sharing the same visual experience without a word being spoken. Social communication has begun.

The baby will observe and learn about the caregiver from the caregiver's reactions to the object, and in turn the caregiver will observe and learn something about the baby from the baby's reactions. They will use joint attention to get to know each other. This kind of joint attention is called *reactive joint attention*. This form of joint attention starts as early as 5 months after the baby is born.

Later on the baby will initiate episodes of joint attention by attracting the caregiver's attention to a certain thing or event. This is the baby showing something to the caregiver for the pleasure of sharing the experience, getting attention and learning from the more experienced caregiver. This is called *initiated joint attention*. It can be first noted in a toddler, a little older than one year of age.

In the course of social development, eye contact comes before and is needed for the appearance of joint attention. Joint attention is perhaps the most pivotal event in the social development of children. The failure to develop joint attention is a critical marker for the development of ASD. We will hear more about joint attention many times thorough this book.

Causes of ASD

The infant or toddler who fails to develop socially will end up with ASD. But why does this failure happen? People have such a strong and inherent need to communicate with each other, so how can it happen a child will fail to develop this capacity?

We know the capacity to communicate is underpinned by genetic factors. For instance, there seems to be inherent differences between the sexes. Girls, regardless of their cultural upbringing, prefer playing socially with their dolls and similar toys while boys prefer playing physically with things and objects.

In my medical office I have old-fashioned exam tables with big black knobs sticking out on the sides of each of the tables. They are perfectly visible to any child who comes in to be examined. Most boys notice them and want to play with them. To boys, these kinds of objects beg to be handled. In contrast, they do not seem to capture the attention of the girls.

Later on as teenagers, girls often seem unable to stop talking and interacting with friends while boys often prefer to keep their feelings and thoughts to themselves. Social communication and social networks seem inherently more important to females. Not surprisingly then boys are four times more likely to develop ASD than girls. In children with Asperger's, a high functioning form of ASD, I have seen the sex ratio quoted as high as 17 boys to one girl. It appears some genetic difference between the sexes affects our interest in social communication, making boys more prone to this condition.

There are other strong pieces of evidence supporting a genetic linkage to ASD that will be discussed in Chapter 5. The study of twins has shown there are many capacities of our minds that have a demonstrated genetic linkage so it is hardly surprising social communication would be included on this list. Is genetics the whole story? If we understood all the genes involved and how they interacted, would we then have the complete explanation for ASD?

Autism Prevalence: On the Rise

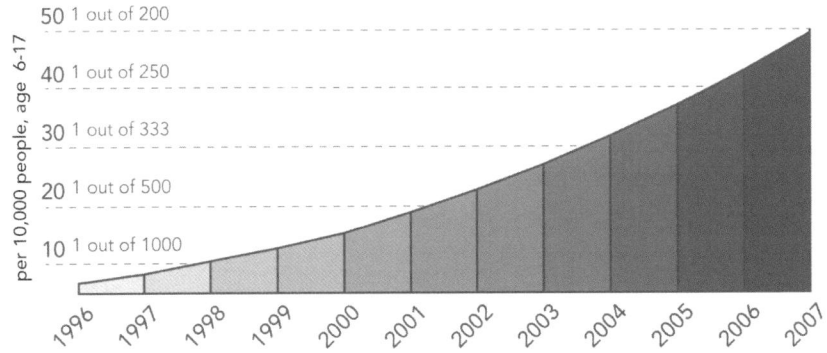

I think not. Genetics cannot explain why ASD is, by and large, a disorder of the modern age whose incidence has been rapidly and alarmingly increasing for the past 50 years. The Autism and Developmental Disabilities Monitoring Network has reported a staggering 57% increase in the prevalence of autism spectrum disorders in just the four years between 2002 and 2006.

Obesity: A Parallel Problem

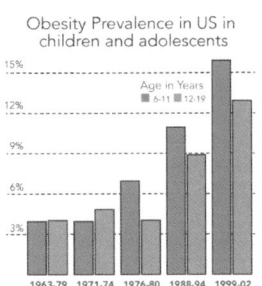

Using modern diagnostic criteria, the incidence of ASD in 1950 was recently estimated to be four per ten thousand children. Today it is about one per one hundred or less children. That is a 25-fold increase. This rise isn't just a question of increasing awareness or earlier diagnosis; there is a genuine increase in the frequency of the condition. Like children with obesity and diabetes, there is something connected to modern life affecting our children in a very harmful way.

The genetic makeup of our species has not changed during this time; the 23,000 or so genes that make up the genome of our species changes very very slowly. Aside from some mixing, we are practically the same species genetically we were 100,000 years ago. Genetics alone cannot explain this surge in the number of children affected by ASD or for that matter childhood obesity. Something in the environment is interacting with a genetic predisposition to cause ASD in the modern era.

Introduction to the Integrated Theory of Autism

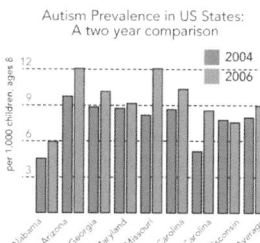

If the cause of ASD is 90% genetic, as many investigators believe, then how do we explain the dramatic increase in the number of children affected by ASD in the last 50 years, and especially in the last 20 years? This is the basic paradox that has puzzled investigators. The Integrated Theory of Autism explains this paradox by showing how an environmental factor, the growing presence of one-way communication in the nursery, has led to ever increasing numbers of children with ASD. The Integrated Theory of Autism reflects the author's understanding of the forces that cause a child to become autistic.

Each child is born with a certain gender and a blend of genetic tendencies to prefer social versus self-communication. From the time of birth, the infant will encounter experiences that either block or encourage one of these tendencies. Infants today are surrounded with *objects* of compelling interest, especially those infants born to technologically sophisticated well-off parents. These parents can buy all the videos, gadgets, and toys they think might help their children become smarter, such as videos from the *Baby Einstein* series. The experiences the infant has with these videos are a pleasurable form of *one-way communication*. However, ***one-way communication encourages self-involvement at the <u>expense of social development</u>***. This is the core idea of The Integrated Theory of Autism.

This increasing exposure to one-way communication by various devices in the nursery has pushed many otherwise normal children towards self-involvement and has simultaneously blocked the development of normal social communication during the critical first year of life.

The initial failure to form social connections with other people during this period of time sets up a chain reaction of subsequent social failures accounting for much of the clinical picture of ASD. The direct result of excessive self-involvement accounts for the rest of the picture.

The recent invasion of these kinds of experiences into the life of otherwise normal infants is the previously unexplained environmental factor that resolves the paradox. This is the factor that is leading to the dramatic increase in the incidence of ASD in modern life. I call this hypothesis *The Integrated Theory of Autism* because it integrates the effects of the one-way communication, an environmental factor, and genetics in the causation of ASD. The theory also accounts for all the clinical features of ASD.

Where the eyes go the soul follows.

So the question of what is causing ASD becomes tied to the phenomenon of where the infants' eyes, and therefore their attention, are directed. Do they follow their caregiver's eyes to shared experiences? Or do their eyes follow television, video screens and talking toys, so much a part of modern life in the nursery, to solitary experiences. Watching eyes and where they go is a basic part of social intercourse and joint attention. Where the eyes go, the mind, body and soul follows.

Why my Child?

Many people reading this book have a child they know in their family who has ASD. They have the seen the cost of this condition first hand. The cost is heavy with heartbreak, family disruption, and in the end lost-opportunity. The question that always circles overhead in the daily struggle of life with a child with ASD is why. Why did this happen to him? Could I have prevented this?

They look around and see their friends and family members raising their children in much the same way as they have. They think maybe it could be genetic, as many experts say. Maybe one uncle was a bit odd, maybe not. He certainly did not have ASD. What has happened?

The experts all disagree on why ASD happens. The only thing they agree on is the mysterious nature of ASD.

I believe The Integrated Theory of Autism solves this mystery.

We are all born a little different from each other, thanks to the makeup of our genetic material. As I said before, we differ in our interest in objects versus social relationships. Some of us find more pleasure in playing with things and some more in socializing. Infants from the beginning are the same.

These tendencies are not set in stone. What happens every day in an infant's life is important. They have emerged into a bewildering world and have so much to learn in the first year of life. They do not always appear to be learning but they are. It can be hard to see because their channels of communication are so restricted during the first year of life.

But they have ways of telling you what they like and what they do not. Make your baby happy and you will do that action again. Make your baby cry and you want to cry yourself. Babies have ways of training you.

Now suppose you have given birth to one of those infants that likes objects and things. In the old days, some 50 years ago, it would have been no big deal. He would enjoy his rattle but at the end of the day, the rattle can only rattle. It does not have a face with eyes, it cannot sing or talk Motherese, it does not move or change form or color. At the end of the day, he would prefer his caregiver's company and the social interaction that would bring into his life. He would let you know this by crying and fussing when you left his room. And you would never want to leave him alone.

Today, objects such as televisions, videos, and talking toys present real competition to caregivers in capturing their infant's attention and interest. If your baby really likes these things, he will let you know, and pretty soon he will be spending many contented hours in the company of these objects, objects that can't talk with him, can't give him kisses, can't touch him, and can't really help him become a part of this very social world we all live in. This is how I believe ASD develops and this is the subject of my book.

As mysterious as ASD seems today to many investigators, the Sudden Infant Death Syndrome (SIDS), was even more mysterious as recently as 20 years ago. Just like ASD, gender and some genetic factors seemed to be part of the explanation. Just like ASD, it strikes at infants during the first year of life. It was baffling. Infants would be found dead in their cribs for no apparent reason. Finally someone noticed that infants dying from SIDS were mostly found sleeping on their bellies surrounded by pillows. When these practices were changed almost overnight SIDS deaths were cut by half.

Such a simple change, easy to do, has saved the lives of many infants. Could the story with ASD turn out to be much the same? Could a simple change in how we amuse our infants, one that is easy to do, save thousands and thousands of children from ASD? Read on and I think you will come to agree with me that The Pied Pipers of Autism need to be eliminated from the lives of our infants and toddlers for now and forever.

Structure of the book.

This book is broken up into three parts. The first three chapters discuss the nature of ASD. Being a family physician by training and practice, I take the broad inclusive perspective physicians in my field use to understand any medical issue.

On one level, we try to see the problem in the context of the society the patient is a part of. In ASD, this is a very important perspective and is the subject of my first chapter on social networks. Then, we also try to understand the clinical findings that help identify a patient with this condition. That is the subject of the second chapter.

Drilling down, we then look at what is altering the function of the affected organ and causing the clinical findings. In the case of ASD, this organ is the brain, the most remarkable organ in our body and one in which our knowledge is exploding. Chapter Three goes into some detail about the functioning and development of the brain, especially as it concerns learning and ASD. To me, there is no understanding of ASD without at least a brief exploration of these three areas.

The next section of the book, with chapters on gender, genetics, social environment and TV video and toys, deals with the various causes and their respective contributions to the cause of ASD.

Finally, the book ends with a chapter on treatment followed by the concluding chapter, where I discuss the all-important topic of prevention and speculate on future directions of research.

In between these chapters are vignettes about Otto by family members.

Throughout the book I use the pronoun 'he' in place of the more awkward 'he or she' as a convenience. I do not mean to neglect the importance of girls with ASD. This is a problem for both sexes.

If you run across terms you are not familiar with, consult the glossary, in the back of the book.

Since this book has been made for both e-book and print-on-demand formats, at times the page spacing around illustrations seems odd. Please forgive this appearance.

Please join me in this exploration of the nature, causes, prevention, treatment and future of ASD.

About Otto- One
Roseli's Story

In Roseli's words…

I am one of Otto's aunts, the oldest one of three sisters. Naturally it was expected that I would be generating the first grandchild in the family. Unfortunately my first marriage ended up broken in the early beginning and my hopes to have a baby were very tiny. So, when my sister announced her pregnancy I was happy for her and my brother in law. I felt as if I was the mother-to-be.

My sister was in Brazil and I was living here in the USA. I could not see her pregnant but I talked to her through phone and emails as much as I could. Otto is the first grandchild in both sides of the family; he is the first nephew for my brother-in-law's sisters, too. We all had a lot of anxiety and expectations.

My first opportunity to meet Otto was when he was almost two years old. My sister was pregnant and almost due with my second nephew Erik, Otto's brother. I arrived in Brazil with a desperate need to hug and kiss my little nephew. All I wanted was to spend time with him, play with him, and give him lots of love. Somehow things didn't go just quite right.

Otto seemed very indifferent to everyone. He was strongly attached to my father, his grandfather, and easily absorbed in this TV show called Baby Einstein. My sister was amazed with Otto's deep interest in the TV. Otto was saying words in English and in Portuguese and we all were mesmerized by this ability.

I remember him sitting in front of the TV and being so absorbed into the show that nothing I tried made him laugh or deviated his attention. In fact, I was so disappointed because the only thing that I was able to do was to make him upset with me. Exactly the opposite of what I was trying to do.

Well, I thought once again, I am so far away from him, this is our first encounter, he does not know who I am and it is natural that he does not want to play with me.

- Roseli

Author's Comments

Otto's mother and father are both highly educated. His mother, Rosangela, has a PhD in biochemistry and does research at the highly respected University of Brazil in San Paulo. His father, Marcio, works as a system analyst in the same institution. Marcio's parents are both professors. So Otto was born into a family with high expectations for his future. Both parents are quite comfortable with technology. The apartment they were living in had a large screen television and a computer, both of which engaged Otto's attention a good part of the day from the beginning of his life.

Otto picked up his English words from television and videos, not from his family, although both parents speak English well. The English words and phrases in his speech were snippets he learned from television and videos. He was not engaging in two-way conversations with people.

Otto's self-absorption prevented him from understanding the nature of a visit from an aunt and was deeply disappointing for Roseli.

Chapter One
Social Networks

What would our lives be like without someone to talk with, someone to listen to us, in other words without conversation or social interaction? What if we were isolated and could not communicate with our families, our friends, and all the social groups we care about? What would our lives being missing? Everything that matters? How much would we miss the social networks we are a part of?

ASD is marked by a failure of infants and children to develop social communication to varying degrees. The infant or child with ASD lives a solitary life with too much self-communication. The self-communication may be an internal monologue or, in situations where the child does not develop language, just a series of inner thoughts.

A person with this disorder finds it difficult or even impossible to participate in the social networks surrounding him. But in terms of this book, what are social networks and why are they so important in the understanding of ASD? In this chapter I will discuss how humans form social networks large and small using both two-way and one-way communication.

When two-way communication stops working it is no longer possible to participate in social networks. It is difficult to understand what it means to have ASD without first looking at social networks and how they enrich our lives. These same networks are missing from the lives of people with ASD. That is the also subject of this chapter.

I find most people are more or less completely oblivious to the importance of social networks in their lives and unaware of the vital role they play.

Just as we take the oxygen in the air for granted, we also assume our social networks will always be there connecting us to the important people of our lives. Just as we are a part of these networks, they are a part of us. They are a part of our thoughts, beliefs, hopes, and fears during every day of our life although we hardly give a second thought about how they work and how they help form our personal identities and histories. In a real sense, they bind us to our recent and distant past history and our future hopes and expectations.

Some of what I say will seem self-evident or basic, seemingly unrelated to ASD. I ask for your patience. Everything I am saying in this chapter in the end ties together with the rest of the book to form what I hope is a rich picture of ASD and the role of communication in this disorder.

One of the topics in this chapter is about how people with ASD have a difficult time understanding what is going on in the minds of people around them. This is a two-way street. Most people have a hard time understanding how people with ASD see things, their point of view. After reading this chapter and this book, I hope you will have a better understanding how the people in the social networks that surround a child with ASD appear to him.

What Are Social Networks?

Social networks are a hot topic today; the internet has made it easier to make connections with people from all over the world. There has been a great deal of study on the shape of social networks, with charts of who communicates with whom, and how things, such as illnesses or information, spread throughout a social network of any given shape. I am going to take a different look at social networks, focusing on the meaning social networks have in our lives.

Communication- Sharing

Communication is the process of sharing something with some other being. That something can be an object, some food, a sound, words, a kiss, a touch, or a thousand other things. As long as it is intended to be received and understood by some other being and to affect that other being in some intended way, it is communication. The sender has an intention and the receiver has a way of decoding that intention.

All social species such as parrots, ants, bees, and primates communicate as a way of coordinating activities including courtship, mating, defense, food collection, and caring for their young. This is beneficial for the survival of the social network as a whole.

The price of this coordination is often harmful to any one member of these groups or social networks. It is clear individual members are often willing to take risks for the greater good of the group. A great deal of thought and study has gone into this area in order to understand how natural selection and evolution work in social species. I will not discuss this fascinating area but will address my thoughts to human social networks and how they develop and the purposes they serve.

Social communication enables the sharing of common interests between people. It is the means by which all social relationships are formed and maintained.

This starts as a newborn baby with the first channel of communication, eye contact. Joint attention follows later on, as early as five months of age. Joint attention is when both the baby and the caregiver share the experience of seeing the same object or event.

Like bricks are for buildings, the joint attention experience is the building block for all social relationships that follow. The reciprocal sharing of attention with the other important people in our life never stops and forms the key events in the creation and sustenance of all social networks. As we grow our interests change and develop. Our means of communication likewise become more diverse and sophisticated. But it is always the same joint attention experience starting in infancy that ties us together.

Social communication then starts with the joint attention experiences of the baby. The experience of a baby and their caregiver sharing eye contact while looking at a novel toy leads directly to political parties, religions, orchestras, and every kind of enterprise we as adults participate in. As such, social networks can and do form around any shared interest. It is sad but people with ASD have great difficulties making these social connections starting from the time of infancy.

Humans are a unique species. When I was younger and studied biology in high school, there was a long list of things that made humans almost completely unlike any other species on the planet. We were taught to think humans were the culmination of evolution, which fit in nicely with what we were learning in our religious education.

During my lifetime I have watched the list of traits separating humans from mere monkeys and other species gradually become shorter and shorter. It has become clear man's separation from the other species on earth is more a question of degree than any complete separation.

But here are two areas where humans really seem to differ substantially from other species: the abilities of children to develop fluency in language and facility in complex social behavior. These abilities enable us to form very complex long lasting social networks. Joint attention seems to be vital to the development of both skills.

Shared History

A Social Network Needs a Shared Past and an Imagined Shared Future.

Social communication and common interest are required to form a social network. But it is not enough. What makes a social network different from some random people talking together about today's football game?

For the purposes of this book, when I refer to a social network, I am referring to a collection of people who not only communicate in the present but have also shared communications in the past and believe they will continue to do so in the future. They have a shared common interest which has endured up until now. They believe this common interest will go on into the uncertain future. This is the kind of social networks that matters and gives meaning to life.

A group of students taking a certain class together can form a social network. The common interest and subject of conversation could be the teacher, the other students, or even the subject matter. The class has a beginning and an ending, so during the term of the class, they have a shared history and an anticipated shared future. However, at the end of the class, the students will no longer have an anticipated future. When this happens the social network will usually dissolve and disperse.

As a physician, my chosen specialty is family practice. As a family physician, I am expected and privileged to be almost a part of my patients' families, at times even their extended families. The relationship is open-ended, lasting until either I retire or until my patients leave the area or change insurances. I have taken care of some patients since I delivered them to this world over twenty years ago. This is a social network. It has a shared past and an expected future.

On the other hand, the urgent care provider and his patient are not part of a social network. There is interaction and communication between the urgent care provider and the patient during the visit, but there is no expectation of any future relationship. This is not a social network in the sense I am referring to in this book. Although the service provided by both providers might be practically the same, the relationship is quite different and it is the expectation of future social communication makes the difference.

The Family and the Kinship Group- Our First Social Networks

Our First Social Networks

In humans, the basic social network we are born into is the family. After all, everyone has a biological mother at birth. The family in this sense refers to the parents and children. The family has a history, depending on the culture, which may go back generations. Often deceased family members form a part of the remembered history of the family. At times, they are imagined to be still in communication with the living. The closer we were to the deceased family members, the more we feel their absence. Grief, in a way, is how we cope with a social network torn apart, sometimes by death.

The family is usually part of a larger kinship group consisting of various genetically-related people such as grandparents, cousins, nephews and the like. This is an example of a smaller social network, the *family*, within a larger social network, the *kinship group*. The family and kinship group often share resources and provide protection to their members.

The basic form of communication in this kind of network is face-to-face, two-way communication, or some variation thereof. In modern times, when the kinship group is often geographically spread apart, other two-way channels of communication are used such as the telephone and internet to stay in touch. But even in this situation, when the members are widely dispersed, they hope the kinship group will outlast the life of any one member.

The family and kinship groups as social networks are characterized by deep trust, unwavering loyalty, long-lasting relationships, and two-way reciprocal communication. The sharing is so generous it does not even feel like sharing. It is the setting where reproduction and child-rearing takes place. Without reproduction and child-rearing, the family and the kinship group have no long term future.

Learning within the family takes place mostly by observation and imitation, but also by rewards and punishments. It is the family that feels the disconnection of the child with ASD most acutely.

Infants and children normally feel safe and secure in their families, and they hopefully feel wanted and loved. How does this come about? The sense of connection and security is provided by the two-way communication and the joint attention the child finds in the normal family. The child with ASD is cut off from these sources of comfort because they do not participate in joint attention or two-way communication easily.

Another source of security for the child is the memory of the experiences he has had within the family. Hopefully the child with ASD lives in a family with a history of safety and nurturing. The child with ASD may feel these ties built by experience very strongly; this is especially true given his inability to form social connections outside the family. As such, children with ASD develop strong connections and loyalties to their families.

Social Networks Beyond the Kinship Group

Beyond the family and kinship groups, we come to larger groupings of people communicating with each other. These groups are tied together by sharing a common set of thoughts and beliefs that form the *culture* of the group.

 The power of this culture is very formidable. People united by common beliefs and patterns of thought are capable of great feats of cooperation. Everyone in the group who shares the same culture understands to a certain degree how everyone else in the group thinks and how they can be expected to act.

We make sense of the world around us through the eyes of our culture. For instance, what do we think of the sun? Any culture in the world, from so called "primitive cultures" to our modern culture, will have an explanation of the sun's behavior that will make sense, more or less, in the context of all the other beliefs and thoughts in that culture. Ideas that are inconsistent with current cultural beliefs simply do not seem to make sense though cultural beliefs can change gradually or rapidly.

When I was young, smoking was widely accepted, and as a child everywhere I went there were ashtrays and people smoking. If a restaurant owner would have forbidden smoking back then, people would have thought he was either very silly or flat-out nutty. He would have clearly been the subject of ridicule, one of the strongest actions a culture can take to enforce its boundaries. Over time cultural attitudes shifted as people learned more about the dangers of smoking. Today, in California anyway, a restaurant owner who permits smoking can be fined or even arrested, which is another way a culture enforces its boundaries.

In modern society anyone might belong to any number of social networks such as churches, companies, schools, political groups and so on. These are groups with a history, shared futures and common ideas. As opposed to the family social network, much of the communication in these groups is one-way and hierarchical; from the leader or leaders to the members of the group. The trust and loyalty can be strong, but not to the degree one would find in the social network we call family.

The larger groups often have rituals and tests to affirm the loyalty of its members. These tests will most often require two-way face-to-face communication. People may be interviewed or asked to take a vow or tested on their knowledge of the ideas of the group. These procedures are intended to build mutual trust. People with ASD may have difficulty with the two-way form of communication required in this kind of situation.

Theory of Mind- Mind Reading in Social Networks

Social communication is the activity that ties all these groups together. It is a dance in which each performer first forms a mental representation of the other performer and each person mentally anticipates the next move of the other person based on what they know about that person and their common history.

I have always been amazed by the women in my life who can remember a conversation I had with them years ago, almost word for word. This kind of memory is called episodic memory, memory for the episodes of our lives.

Somewhere in their brains is a model of me, and everything I have said in their presence somehow fits into that model. Some bits of gossip also form a part of this model; people love to talk about other people when they are not around as a way of developing a better mental model of that person. Everything we hear, see and remember about a person goes into this representation in our minds of that person.

This ability is called *theory of mind*. It is being able to picture what is going on in the mind of someone else, to see things from their point of view. It is like being able to read someone else's mind, and it is an area in which people with ASD have great difficulty. To be clear, theory of mind is no theory at all. It refers to the ability we have to picture what is going on in other people's minds, who they are, what they intend to do, and what motivates them or shall we say what make them tick.

How does a child develop this ability? It comes through repeated episodes of eye contact and joint attention starting with the infant's caregiver. By looking at the eyes of another person the infant can determine what the other person is looking at. By looking and listening to the reaction of the other person to that shared visual experience, the infant and child learns to understand what is going on inside the other person's mind, literally the other person's point of view.

Over years of continual practice with different people and in different social settings, the child will develop this skill to the point where it becomes automatic, very fast, and seemingly intuitive. Conversation will be flowing and seamless. Other people will enjoy the company of such a sociable child. The pleasure of attention the child gets and gives in these episodes of joint attention drives this dynamic forward.

But what about a child who does not find pleasure in social communication? Where would such a child find the motivation to engage in social interactions again and again? The child might be more interested in objects or videos that do not require social communication. Instead of building a theory of mind for the people in his social network, the child might be enjoying picturing how certain objects or things act. In the end a child who does not or cannot engage in social communication cannot easily build a theory of mind about other people.

What is so important about having a theory of mind? A theory of mind is the mental model a person has of what other people are thinking. The model allows a child to predict and anticipate the future behavior of other people. Trust is the key issue here; a child is more or less totally defenseless and being able to predict who to trust and who not to trust is a matter of vital importance.

A child's ability to form a theory of mind, to understand the intentions of others, allows trust to develop in the course of social relationships. It makes other people seem less mysterious. You could almost say a child becomes an adult when they no longer need the protection of the family in performing this function.

This area of study, the theory of mind, has been thoroughly investigated in children with ASD. By the age of four normal children will pass the

Sally-Anne false belief test. In this test, the child is told the following scenario:

> *Sally places a ball in a basket and leaves the room. Anne comes in the room and moves the ball to a box.*

The question then is: *where will Sally look for the ball when she returns to the room?* The child who has developed a theory of mind will say the basket, while children with ASD who do not have a fully formed theory of mind will say the box.

For some time this failure to form a theory of mind was thought to be the fundamental and essential defect in ASD. It is now understood that ASD starts during the first year of life, well before the theory of mind develops even in normal children. Rather, the failure of the development of theory of mind is part of a sequence of social development skills that do not develop normally or at all in children with ASD.

Theory of Culture- Understanding Your Culture

Each person likewise has what I will call a *theory of culture* that performs the same function as a theory of mind, but for the larger social networks they are a part of. The theory of culture is not a theory, but an ability we have to understand and predict how other people in our culture will react to any given situation or action. A culture is a social network of people who share many of the same ideas, loyalties, and beliefs. These ideas are also referred to as the 'culture' of that social network. This usage is a bit confusing but it is how this word is used in English. So the theory of culture allows us in a sense to 'mind read' our cultural social network.

People who share the same religion or who are citizens of the same country are all a part of a larger social network. They share a common history and hold common beliefs. The *theory of culture* each member carries in their minds allows them to anticipate the reactions of the people who are members of the culture to any action they may care to act out.

For instance, as a physician, I am part of a social network of other physicians. I know this group expects me to take care of my patients in a caring, thoughtful fashion. I understand if I violate that trust I stand to be condemned or ridiculed by this social network.

Knowledge and understanding of the values and beliefs of the group is often acquired by one-way communication. This is unlike the family where joint attention and two-way communication are the rule. We learn about our culture from people outside of the family, such as teachers, religious leaders and other role models, as well as from shared stories, books, artworks, drama, TV shows, newspapers and so on.

In the last 300 years or so, there has been an explosion of the availability of one-way communication. This exposure to new ideas has transformed modern civilization. Still, most normal behavior for a given culture is learned at home from two-way face-to-face social communication with other family members.

A person with ASD is more or less cut off from two-way communication and thus forms either no theory of culture or a very idiosyncratic version thereof. The child with ASD often behaves in ways that are culturally unacceptable which can subject the child and the family to ridicule. This is very disturbing for the family. The child at times engages in dangerous behavior.

Adolescence is a period in life when odd behavior is strongly scorned. All adolescents want and need to be to be accepted by their peers in their social networks which are often very cliquish. This makes this period of development very difficult and painful for people with ASD.

There is growing understanding of the problem of ASD in our culture. The cultural attitudes towards people with ASD are in a period of flux. Television, newspapers, and even books are spreading new information and ideas about ASD widely throughout our culture. People are learning about ASD indirectly by one-way communication.

As the prevalence of ASD continues to increase, more and more families will be directly impacted by a family member with this condition. As such they will be forced to confront the nature of this disorder directly, face-to-face. These experiences will also gradually change our culture's attitudes and ideas about ASD.

Every person in modern society can belong to any number of social network groups. The key factors to forming a social network are communication, common interests, a shared history and an expectation for future communication. There is usually a mixture of one and two-way communication in these groups. Participating in social networks gives our lives interest, meaning and purpose. People with ASD often have the capability to identify with and develop strong bonds to appropriate social networks, including family and country. It is the act of two-way reciprocal communication that starts as joint attention in the nursery they find difficult to understand and uninteresting.

Families with a child with ASD sooner or later develop concerns over what is going wrong with their beloved child. Why are they not fitting into their family or other social networks? For Otto, his parents realized there was a problem when he was observed to play alone away from the other children in nursery school. In the next chapter, I will discuss the characteristic features of the child with ASD.

About Otto – Two
Roseli's Story Continued

When Otto was about four years old I went back to visit again, this time with Lenny [the author]. This time I had some heads up from my sister that something was different with Otto. The first thing was, he was potty trained but it seemed that he had forgotten. Was he calling for attention? Was he jealous of his brother? What was going on with this boy?

Talking to my sister in Brazil I found out that there was more to the picture. Otto refused to participate in the group activities with other children at his pre-school group. Otto isolated himself frequently and did not play with toys. Otto had some obsessions, for instance, the red color clothes, the movie *Cars* from Disney, the character McQueen. Otto knew all the dialogues of the movie *Cars* in Portuguese and English. I doubt that there is a person in this world that has watched the movie *Cars* more than Otto.

Again I tried to engage Otto in conversation, to play with him, to show my love, to hug and to kiss but again it was not the warm and fuzzy relationship I expected. At the same time I was reading books about autism. I don't know why exactly but I had just finished my nursing school and was reading some books for fun and I came across books with stories about children with Asperger's syndrome and their parent's struggle.

When we were leaving Brazil, inside the plane Lenny and I were talking about Otto. Lenny said he thought perhaps Otto did not like me. This comment was a knife stabbing my heart. I love Otto like he was my own child. I felt his rejection, of course, but he had no reason to not like his auntie. At least I thought I was being good to him.

I showered him with all the McQueen clothes and toys that I could afford. Although I was far away, I called Brazil weekly to ask how my boys were doing. I still do that, if I cannot reach my sister (Rosangela), I at least call my parents to know how my children are. Anyway, I remember thinking I cannot say for sure Otto whether likes me or not but I know that something is wrong and I suspected that Otto had autism. I remember telling Lenny that it seemed to me that Otto had Asperger's syndrome.

Author's Comments

The power of kinship social networks is awesome. Despite the physical separation of thousands of miles, Roseli felt Otto's social detachment acutely. Otto at this time is nearly 4 years old and there is still only a suspicion that something is wrong. Looking backwards it is easy to see he had a real problem at this time. This is one the paradoxes of ASD. The involvement with television, video, talking toys in the first year of life sets off a time bomb that will gradually detonate over the ensuing years.

Chapter Two
The Spectrum of Autism Spectrum Disorders

What do you look for if you suspect a child you know might have ASD? Why is it so hard to detect in the first year of life? Why does the early failure of social development lead to full blown ASD later on? Why do kids with ASD show such disturbing symptoms as flapping, tantrums, fixed routines, narrow fixed interests, or fascination with objects? In this chapter I will briefly review the clinical picture of ASD from the severe side of the spectrum to the almost normal and I will try to answer these puzzling questions about ASD.

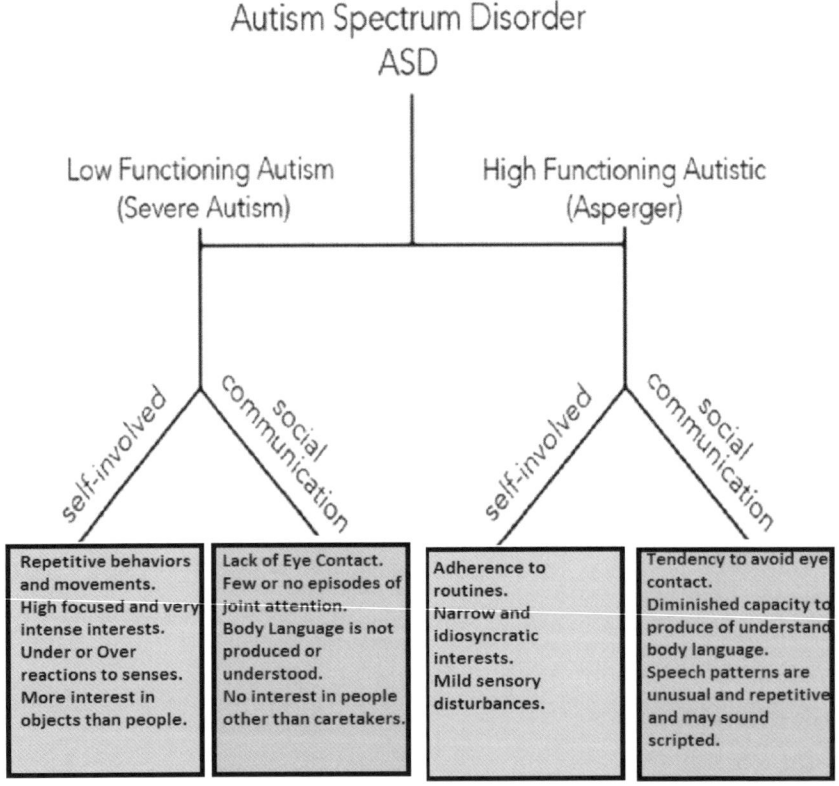

There are two conditions that are grouped together to form *Autism Spectrum Disorder*. The first and most severe is autism itself. The second is Asperger's Syndrome, in which language function develops at the usual developmental time.

Description of the Criteria in the DSM-V for ASD

Children with ASD do not always neatly fit in one diagnostic box. As the name 'spectrum' suggests, there is a range of findings from the severe to the almost normal. The clinical picture can change, and a child can go from being labeled with one condition to another over time. In fact, in the proposed revision of the DSM-V, the book that is the authority on the classification of psychiatric disorders, the separation of Autism, Asperger's, and Pervasive Development Disorder is discarded entirely and all these disorders are simply combined into one category: Autism Spectrum Disorder (ASD), with different levels of severity. It is important to realize the high-functioning end of the spectrum blends into normal or, as it is frequently called, *neurotypical* behavior or simply typical behavior.

Two sets of criteria are used to diagnose ASD in the proposed DSM-V. The first set of criteria describes the various manifestations of impairment in communication and social interaction found in this condition. As described in the DSM-V these criteria include the following: Eye contact is limited or absent, while body language such as gestures and facial expressions are not produced and not understood to varying degrees.

Language communication skills are likewise delayed and are often limited or absent. Language use may sound scripted, and the child may simply repeat what they heard last. Conversation is not initiated and the normal ebb and flow of reciprocal conversation is limited or absent. The child will show little interest in other humans other than their caregivers; the child will also fail to make and sustain friendships and will not engage in shared imaginary or pretend play. He may also not respond to his name or he may refer to himself in the third person.

All these deficits revolve around the failure to develop social communication. I will call these criteria the *social communication criteria*.

The second set of criteria describes the restrictive and repetitive behaviors found in this condition. These include repeating specific body movements, speaking certain words or phrases again and again, eating the same foods, watching the same videos or shows and so forth. These criteria also include distress when these routines and repetitive behaviors are forced to change. Furthermore, interests are highly focused and very intense. Under- and overreactions to sensory stimuli such as noise, heat, cold, or pain are also often seen in ASD.

All these criteria revolve around the self-involvement and self-stimulation so I will call these criteria the *self-involvement criteria*.

Factors Affecting the Expression of the Criteria for ASD

There are three main factors that affect which of the different criteria a child with ASD will express. The first is the severity of the condition itself. That is to say, to what degree is the child locked out of the social world and locked into his private world. The second is the level of cognition or the general intelligence of the child. This a tricky area to actually measure since language skills, which comprise a large part of most IQ tests, are often affected by ASD itself. That being said, the more debilitating cases of autism tend to be found in children who are cognitively challenged.

The third factor is the developmental stage. The child being evaluated for ASD is naturally compared to other children of the same age. However the pace of development can differ from one child to another. Different behaviors are appropriate for different developmental stages.

Development can be looked at as being normal, simply delayed, prematurely stopped, or going in an entirely wrong direction. A child may be behaving appropriately for his developmental stage but not for his age. In ASD, while development takes place over time, the pathway it takes is not shaped nearly as much by the surrounding social environment as with neurotypical children. The child with ASD will tend to make his own unique pathway leading to the confusing array of behaviors and stims found in children with this condition.

As children grow up, their social communication abilities develop increasing complexity with new abilities being built on top of ones previously acquired.

Scaffolding and development of Social Communication

- **13-18 years** Complex interactions with peers. Higher levels of integration with outside social networks.
- **7-13 years** Start of integration with outside social networks. Friendships.
- **4-7 years** Advancing imitation and pretending with role playing. May have best friend.
- **2-4 years** Early stage of imaginative play and Theory of Mind appears. Comforts other child.
- **1-2 years** Gesturing and Pointing; Initiated Joint Attention appears; Turn taking in conversation; Plays by self.
- **6-12 months** JOINT ATTENTION APPEARS. Reciprocal emotional signaling. Baby repeats actions for caretaker's approval.
- **3-6 months** Reacting to Eye Gaze and caretaker's attention; Motherese starts with reciprocal imitation.
- **0-3 months** Attracted to Faces; Bonding to caretaker with crying and comforting. Eye contact.

This cascade of development, one ability building on another, is called *scaffolding*. The young infant with ASD may have a delay or failure in first establishing eye contact with its caregiver. Without eye contact, receptive joint attention cannot develop later on in the first year of life. And then without receptive joint attention, initiated joint attention will not be seen at the start of second year of life. Initiated joint attention is when the child starts an episode of joint attention by first getting the caregiver's attention using pointing or some other means.

Following this trajectory, as the child with ASD gets older, he will not develop in turn social imitation, shared pretending, or theory of mind. As you can see, the difference between the child with ASD and a neurotypical child gradually widens.

The net effect is that the difference between normally developing children and those with ASD becomes greater with age. What started out as subtle difference in eye contact has, by the time these children reach school age, developed into a child with an obvious problem who is quite socially isolated from other children. By this point the gap is wide and treatment is quite difficult. Therefore, the hope is to detect ASD as early as possible, when treatment may be much easier.

ASD- Autism

Autism, itself, represents the most severe form of ASD. These children will show a complete avoidance of eye contact, lack of response to all body and facial communication cues, a failure to speak or understand language, and the lack of any interest in people other than their caregivers. They can be fascinated with the movement of objects. They often engage in repetitive movements such as flapping their arms. These repetitive behaviors are often called *stims* by people involved with the care of children with ASD.

They do not imitate the people around them and they don't play imaginary social games. As they grow older, they may develop rudimentary language skills. They are easily frustrated by human contact and may throw tantrums when frustrated in any way. Humans seem to be an unpleasant distraction from their private world of repetitive movement and watching television and video devices. They may become attached to a certain video and want to watch it over and over again often as part of their fixed daily routine. They likewise often prefer the same foods day after day.

As observers, we can have no idea what these children are thinking or what kind of self-communication is going on in their minds since, after all, they are not communicating with us. From brain imaging studies we know their brains do not react to social stimuli such as faces the way neurotypical children do.

Imagine you are the only human being on a strange planet in outer space. There are no humans to talk with on this planet. However, the planet is full of bewildering and powerful beings. You are truly alone and surrounded by these strange beings. This is how Temple Grandin, a recovered autistic, describes the feelings she felt being around people during her childhood. The world the autistic child lives in is scary, full of powerful and incomprehensible people.

It is difficult to test the mental capabilities of children severely affected by ASD since they have seemingly no interest in communicating, let alone cooperating in some sort of test. But they are awake and alert and can demonstrate their needs and preferences at will. What they are thinking clearly does not appear to be connected to the norms of their family or culture. They are apparently incapable and uninterested in forming new social relationships. These children represent the severe end of ASD spectrum.

Children with this more severe form of ASD will frequently have cognitive difficulties. Their language and social communication difficulties are not simply a result of a low IQ, since many children with similarly low IQs develop good language and social skills. Other children with low IQ's often use their social skills to help compensate for their weaknesses in cognition. After all, there are usually two ways to solve any problem, figure it out yourself or ask a friend for help.

ASD- Asperger's Syndrome

On the other end of the ASD spectrum are people with normal language abilities but impaired communication skills. These people carry the diagnosis of Asperger's syndrome after the Austrian pediatrician, Hans Asperger, who first described this condition in 1944.

People with this condition often appear to not empathize with their listeners and may talk endlessly about a given topic in which the listener is not interested, missing the cues that signify disinterest. They may also have abnormal vocal intonations and the normal ebb and flow of conversation may be missing. They may avoid eye contact. The listener may get the impression the person with this form of ASD is carrying on a one-sided conversation and is not really paying attention to the listener.

People with this condition may enjoy attention from other people but seem quite incapable of reciprocating. However, they are verbal and can communicate clearly, and they are quite capable of expressing their thoughts. If anything, they often appear too honest, not knowing appropriate from inappropriate settings and times to share their thoughts with other people.

In addition, they often move awkwardly and have problems with physical coordination. This leads to difficulty playing sports. Team sports involving coordination and social communication will often be beyond the reach of these children.

Since they can communicate, it is easier to test their cognitive abilities. Testing these abilities involves a battery of different scales, each looking at different brain functions, some verbal and some spatial. The child with Asperger's may do spectacularly well in areas related to their intense interests and abysmally in other areas. Not being really a part of the larger cultural social network allows the children with ASD to develop their cognitive abilities in an idiosyncratic narrowly focused fashion.

Often these children are not diagnosed until they are five years of age or older. To their family they may appear a bit odd but more or less normal. They may have special abilities related to their intense interests. It is not until they start attending school, where they have to deal with other children, that their differences become readily apparent. In school settings they often appear withdrawn and are subject to teasing and ridicule by the other children.

Early Findings in ASD

There are early subtle signs in ASD during the first year of life. It is difficult to appreciate these early signs until the child starts displaying abnormalities in communication, such as a delayed ability to talk. This comes long after the critical period for the learning of social communication has passed.

First Birthday Party for a girl with ASD.

Normal children will not start talking until they are over one year old; although before they start talking, they already understand a lot of spoken language. ASD will go undetected in most children until they do not start talking at the appropriate age.

Even so, there are other things that can cause this *mutism*. For one, hearing difficulties can be an issue. In other cases, children will have difficulties with social communication or language usage only outside of their family. Still other children are eager to communicate but use non-verbal means such as body language. But the alarm for autism is often first set off by mutism. By seven or eight years of age, ASD is either apparent or absent.

Interestingly enough, when home videos of children with ASD are reviewed, there are signs of disturbed social communication even at an early age. As these signs become better understood in the medical field and by the general public, it is hoped ASD can be detected and treated earlier. As you will read later in this book, it is my hope that ASD can be prevented entirely by avoiding such activities as watching television and other forms of one-way communication.

Poor eye contact is perhaps the earliest and most telling sign of ASD in a baby. Even as young babies, these children often do not like to play with other family members. They have more interest in objects than people, and often have more interest in the characters seen on video screens than the living faces of their caregivers. They may not exhibit the babbling normally found in young infants. They can appear uncomfortable when held or disturbed, or go quickly from being very passive to very irritable. It is important to understand the signs of ASD can *appear during the first year of life, but they are subtle.*

These signs all deal with the early failure to acquire social communication and, in its place, an excess of self-involvement. The first year of life is the critical period for infants to develop an interest in and a capability for social communication. The subsequent signs of ASD all follow logically and inevitably from this initial failure of social development. As language and other forms of communication fail to develop and obvious behaviors of excess self-involvement and self-stimulation appear, more and more of the DSM-V criteria become expressed by the child.

Development of Social Communication and Affection

As mentioned in the introduction, as early as five months after birth 'joint attention' appears. To recall, these are episodes where the infant and caregiver *react* to an object or an event by looking at the each other's eyes to see where their eyes are in turn looking. Consequently, the caregiver and the infant both know their collective attention is directed at the same thing and each other. This is called *reactive joint attention.*

Later on the normal toddler will *initiate* these episodes by getting his caregiver's attention by pointing, for instance, as the first step in an episode of joint attention. This is called *initiated joint attention.* The failure of the child to develop this latter pattern of behavior is a key early marker of ASD.

Joint attention does not magically appear at six months of life; it is a culmination of a series of encounters between the infant and the caregiver. The key event is the infant's perception and interest in other people, especially his or her caregiver. As the infant develops motor control from the age of 2 to 5 months, it responds to others' gaze with interest or disinterest, pleasure or avoidance. Some infants respond easily and positively to the caregiver's attention, while others have to be *wooed*. This is a delicate dance between the caregiver and the baby, each learning how to please the other.

The caregiver speaks in a special tone and tempo called *Motherese* which attracts the baby's attention. The baby responds by cooing. Motherese is a universal human behavior and is found in all human societies. Anywhere you go in the world, you can recognize the sound of a mother talking to her baby. A very powerful bond develops between infant and caregiver, forming a key social network for both which will last a lifetime.

The next stage in this process is built on the prior one. During the period from 6 to 10 months, the infant develops two-way communication. During this time, the infant will demonstrate via body movements and facial expressions a wider range of emotions such as pleasure, fear or assertiveness.

The caregiver will react to the infant's expressions of emotion and challenge the infant to react back. Smiles will be exchanged. When looking at an object, the infant's gaze will alternate between the caregiver and the object, and the infant will repeat actions that have elicited pleasurable reactions from the caregiver in the past, looking right at the caregiver's face.

The infant starts to observe and learn from the caregiver's reactions how to react to the variety of stimuli that enter the nursery. These reactions transmit the values and ideas of the family and culture that the infant will be a part of. The key sign in this stage is the back and forth connection of eye gazing.

The exchange of touch, particularly by hand, can be a very important channel of communication for the infant, especially if hearing or vision is impaired. In the second half of the first year of life, joint attention appears- opening the door for fuller social and language development. However, by this point in time the child with ASD may be showing a very different pattern of social development.

Development of Self-Involvement Findings in ASD

With that understanding of the social development, we can look at the self-involvement criteria for the diagnosis of Autism Spectrum Disorder proposed in the DSM-V and make sense of what is going on. The children, as we have discussed, have varying degrees of social communication impairment, from profound isolation to almost normal. The self-involvement criteria describe what happens to children who are cut off from their social networks during infancy and early childhood.

A neurotypical infant's interests are shaped and modulated by the reactions of the social networks they are a part of. I would argue this influence never stops, even in adulthood. Would I have this much interest in autism if the culture I lived in did not think it was an important issue? Maybe, or maybe not. A person with ASD will more or less disregard the social value a particular interest might or might not have for other people.

Sensory Findings

In my hometown of Merced, I have been fortunate enough to care for patients from various cultures. When I was delivering a lot of babies I noted how dissimilarly patients from different cultures reacted to the pain of giving birth. At the time, I supposed my patients had learned to express and react to similar degrees of pain from the people around them as children. I still believe this is part of the picture. But now I also think as children and infants as we watch our caregivers and other members of our social networks, we actually learn what sensations feel like.

I recall demonstrating to my little girl how to react when she, for instance, falls. I personally tend to be stoical and generally try to see humor in painful situations, and I will act out this role in front of her when I hurt myself. She watches and imitates me.

My grown-up children react to pain in somewhat the same way as I do. As I said, I think the sensation of pain is partly learned from our caregivers. We learn as children by observation and imitation and through a myriad of joint attention episodes just how to feel, interpret and react to our senses.

Children who are isolated from these shaping forces will acquire deeply idiosyncratic reactions to their senses. Suppose a child hears an odd or unfamiliar noise, such as a siren. A neurotypical child will quickly look at his or her caregiver's eyes (an episode of joint attention) and see how they respond. This is called *social referencing*. The child will learn to react just like their caregiver.

The caregiver's reaction expresses an appropriate reaction for their social network. The infant with ASD, not being able to join in joint attention, will be left to himself to react to the sound however he chooses.

The neurotypical child uses the one-way communication of the siren as a bridge to two-way communication with the caregiver, whereas the child with ASD is stuck in the lonely world of one-way communication. The usual child learns to react just like everyone else in its social network, but the child with ASD reacts independently of social norms because without joint attention, the child cannot learn them. Looking from the point of view of the culture, the child with ASD appears to under- or over- react, but really he is reacting normally to the sound, only independent of the general cultural norms.

Body Movements

Infants and children watch how the people around them move and use their bodies to communicate. They also watch how the people around them walk, climb, dance or do any number of other activities. Through countless episodes of joint attention, infants and toddlers get a lot feedback about their own body movements. This process then shapes all movements infants and toddlers learn.

Is there anything cuter than a baby doing an adult-like movement, such as clapping or walking, for the first time? That feeling reflects the caregiver's great interest in the baby's movements. The day the baby first walks is an important enough landmark that I am sure most mothers promptly report the happy event to all the interested members of their social networks.

Many children with ASD will acquire, for unfathomable reasons, certain preferred motor movements and speech patterns. Body motions produce sensations; that is to say, when you move your arm your brain feels your arm moving. If you pay attention, you can feel the joints and muscles moving and the changes in muscle tension. Ordinarily people do not pay any attention to these sensations. These feelings are called *proprioception*.

Since a child with ASD is not attending to the movements of other people, his attention is free to develop self-interest in the movements of his own body. Without concern for the caregiver's reaction to this behavior, he derives whatever pleasure and comfort this awareness and control of his body movements may give him. A pathway of neural activity, or *neural network*, can develop in the child's brain to support the behavior. This pathway will grow stronger over time with repeated use. This pathway can become a loop, where the end of the behavior repeatedly causes the behavior to start again.

Special Interests, Routines, and Tantrums

Without having much need for social approval, children with ASD are free to focus their minds on their own interests. Not being distracted by other people's reactions, is it surprising their interests become intense?

We all know how much more disturbing loud noises are when we are concentrating or focusing on some activity or thought; they are very startling and annoying. Imagine that you were cut off from social contact and your attention was always intensely focused on your own thoughts. Would intrusive sensory experiences not be bothersome, or even very bothersome?

If you could not communicate well socially, could this kind of intrusive experience drive you into an uncontrollable rage or tantrum? It might. If somehow, despite the great difficulty you have communicating with this strange world you lived in, you had managed to establish some routines that worked for you and someone decided to change them for you, would you not resist these changes?

These are all symptoms you will find in the self-involvement set of criteria for the diagnosis of Autism Spectrum Disorder. Stereotyped movements, excessive adherence to routines, intensely focused interests, repetitive motions or speech, and odd reactions to sensory stimuli are all criteria for ASD in the proposed DSM-V.

This disregard of the reactions of other people means the child with ASD is more or less oblivious to the needs of other family members. They feel free to establish routines out of sync with the rest of the family. For instance, sleep can be a real problem for a family with a child with ASD. To a child with little or no understanding of other people's points of view, three o'clock in the morning seems like just as good a time to play as any other.

The severity of the disorder in the DSM-V is determined by the degree symptoms limit day-to-day life. The lower the child's cognitive ability, the more difficulty he will have in daily life; as such the severity of ASD often correlates with IQ. It is on the Asperger's end of the spectrum that you find children with normal and high intelligence. These children will often do well in daily life and are called 'high-functioning.'

This is the wrong way to measure severity. A child with ASD, especially after years of training, could behave perfectly in a predictable setting but still have practically no ability to make and keep friends, to socialize. He may remain clueless about other people and their points of view. He may have a good, even excellent, adaption to the social network he lives in but the core problem remains the same. Severity should be judged on a scale of social abilities and empathy for other people.

My argument is that the failure social integration into the family is the indirect cause of the self-involvement findings discussed in the DSM-V for ASD. The beginnings of this failure can be detected in children with

ASD as early as six months of age, when joint attention episodes between the caregivers and the infant often first fail to appear.

These changes in the development of social communication in infants and toddlers are reflections of changes in the brains of these children. In the next chapter I will discuss the role of this all important organ.

About Otto – Three
The End of Roseli's Story

My sister began searching for answers to understand Otto's unusual behavior. Unfortunately she had to listen to all kinds of stupid things that people uneducated in the subject of autism have to say. Since family members were connected to Freudian psychologists, my sister started seeing them. All of them blamed Otto's behavior on her eagerness to help her child.

When finally she found a neurologist who observed Otto for thirty minutes, asked some pertinent questions and gave him a diagnosis of Asperger's Syndrome, it was not a relief but a beginning, a sign on the cracked road that all parents with autistic children ride.

It was not a surprise for me when she called me to tell me the doctor's diagnoses. It was a big surprise to the rest of the family. Well, what will happen with Otto now that we know what is going on with him?

My wife Roseli, my daughter Gigi, and my nephew Otto

In Brazil, public or private schools are not prepared for an autistic child having tantrums. They have only one treatment, call our emergency system and put the child in the white jacket. Can you imagine how sad it is to see that happening with your loved child? My sister had to find help as soon as it was possible. Thank God she came across the Son-Rise program and started Otto and Erik, who also received a diagnosis of a milder range in the autism spectrum.

Last time we went to Brazil I was so glad to receive a hug from my loved Otto. He calls me Tia (aunt) Rosie. Now we talk on the phone, he tells me secrets once in a while. He is playing soccer and when he scored a goal and he told me. I am so proud of him. Last month my little Giovanna turned two years old. We had a little cybernetic Skype party for her. My sisters in Brazil met in one house with their children and we sang happy birthday to my little daughter over the internet. To my most splendid surprise, Otto was the one who spent more time talking to us and entertaining my little Gigi, playing peek-a-boo and making her laugh.

Chapter Three
The Brain, Learning, and ASD

To say the brain is a remarkable organ is the height of understatement. Virtually every capability we develop during our life is a reflection of the workings of our brains.

Our understanding of the brain is exploding. Much of this new knowledge has yet to be popularized. I expect many of the ideas and concepts I will share about the brain in this chapter will be unfamiliar and even startling. As this new knowledge percolates through our culture it is sure to change the way we think about ourselves and each other, including the child with ASD

For instance, the monumental changes that take place in the brain during the first year of life were almost completely unknown during my time in medical school. It is now clear during this time period the infant's brain changes dramatically. Trillions of connections are formed. At the same time millions of nerve cells that are not needed are dying. These processes are helping to shape the brain to come.

Then is it any wonder a one-year-old toddler is a long way from a newborn baby. Babies are born with an incredible collection of latent capabilities. These capabilities are the product of their genetic makeup. Since everyone, except identical twins, has different genes, we are born with different strengths and weaknesses in any given capability. Whether the capability actually develops depends on the stimuli the baby receives from their surroundings. In other words, it depends on the details of their life history.

By one year's time these capabilities have started to develop into many different behaviors. These behaviors include such things as walking, talking, dancing, crawling, holding, handling, and social communication. It is these behaviors that make one-year-olds so clearly different from newborns. And what are behaviors? Behaviors are observable manifestations of brain activity. Our brain controls the actions of our body producing these observable behaviors.

Depth Perception- Interplay between the Brain, Genes, and the Surrounding World.

Baby on a Visual Cliff

Even something as important and fundamental as vision is clearly shaped both by inherent capabilities and the environment surrounding the baby. An infant is born without the ability to see stereoscopically; that is to say, they have no depth perception. To them, the world looks blurry and flat. This is an area well studied in young infants.

By watching how these infants react to *visual cliffs*, the observer can tell if they have depth perception or not. A visual cliff is a flat surface that visually appears to suddenly fall off. If the baby has depth perception when it approaches what appears to be the edge of a surface, his heart rate will increase.

Depth perception involves a number of different cues, such as objects blurring in the distance and interpositioning of some objects in front of others; but the main one is the difference in the images between the two eyes. A small difference between the images in each eye, and our very clever brains, allow us to see the world in three dimensions.

But, as I said, we are not born this way. Genetically, at the time of birth, our brains are provided with a huge number of nerve cells called neurons and a basic architecture saying where in the brain certain functions will take place. There is an area of the brain where three dimension vision will be formed, I guess somewhat analogous to a graphic chip in a computer. But the connections from the eyes to this area need to be organized to be functional.

There simply are not enough genes to specify each and every one of the trillions of connections in the brain. So instead our genes specify a competitive process that selects the location of these connections. The process basically follows this rule: Neurons that fire together, or in other words perceive the same stimuli, lie together in the brain. This means the surface of this area of the brain will form microscopic little strips with the right eye's image lying next to the left eye's image.

Since this is a competitive process, you may wonder what happens to the neurons in the brain that do not form a connection. The simple answer to this question is they die or disappear. Part of the process of development of the brain during the first years of life requires the selection of neurons which will prove useful to the brain and the cell death of millions of other neurons that were alive at the time of birth.

You may say what a waste but if you allow me a bit of leeway here, the challenge of designing a brain is to customize it for the user (you and I) and at the same time keep it small enough to fit into our heads. If millions of neurons have to die to serve us better, so be it.

Getting back to three-dimensional vision, nerve impulses coming from <u>both eyes</u> are needed to induce the change in the brain that forms the paired microscopic little stripes I just mentioned. Because of the position of the eyes on our face, each eye sees things at a slightly different angle from the other eye. By the age of three months, infants can combine the images from both eyes so they are looking at the same thing and the brain is forming one image. This is the first step to three-dimensional vision.

Then at some point in time between three and six months, three dimensional vision and depth perception appears. Corresponding to these changes are actual physical changes in the area of the brain processing vision, the visual cortex. The cortex is the outer layer of the brain. You can actually see the changes with a good microscope.

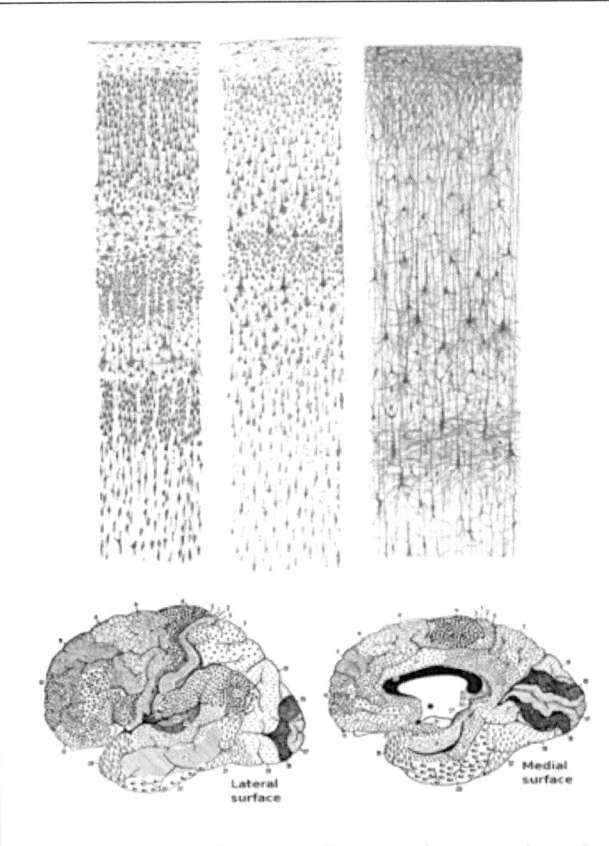

(top) Surface of cortex (bottom) Lateral and medial surfaces of the brain with Brodman's Area numbered

The surface of the brain is organized, as I described, with the images from the right and left eyes right next to each other. Like a layer cake, underneath the surface of the cerebral cortex are a series of layers going down from surface. The layers are composed of columns of different neurons.

Different areas in the brain that do different things have layers that appear different when looked at through a microscope. They were first described by an investigator called Korbinian Brodman who described 51 patterns of layers in different areas in the brain. These areas are called Brodman's areas in his honor.

The processing, that takes the eye images and combines them to give us the picture of our three dimensional world, takes place in the visual cortex called Brodman's areas 17 and 18.

Looking at the top of illustration above, you can see the different layers in three different Brodman's areas. The layers are composed of parallel columns of nerve cells, one next to the other. The columns themselves are stacks of neurons, one neuron above another. Between the neurons is a web of axons, dendrites, and synapses all packed and weaved together to make connections to other neurons.

As a baby acquires depth vision, the appearance of the different layers changes. The neurons with all their axons and dendrites re-arrange. The baby can now see in three dimensions. It is all so amazing.

This process, however, does not happen automatically. If you interfere with normal development by for instance covering one eye, depth perception does not develop. The baby needs the stimuli of visual input from both eyes to the brain to develop depth perception.

There is a window of opportunity during this period of time for the brain to develop depth perception. If this window of time is missed, the opportunity is gone. If vision is restored so both eyes can see later on, depth perception does not usually develop. This area of the brain can no longer be organized in this way. This period of time is called the *Critical Period.* However, thanks to *Brain Plasticity*, meaning the ability of the brain to reconstruct or sort of rewire itself, depth perception can sometimes still be captured later in life with proper training.

You can also find people, who despite being born with two good eyes and an apparently normal brain do not develop depth perception. Somehow they were born with a set of genes that did not allow the development of depth perception. Sometimes through training they, too, can acquire three-dimensional vision, but to do so requires a lot of practice and attention.

Depth perception is a great example of the interaction between development, genetics, and the surrounding world. The brain is the organ most responsible for our integration into the world around us. You could say that is the brain's primary mission. Its proper function depends on a constant interplay of environmental and genetic factors.

At the time of conception we inherit our genes from our parents. These precious genes are a product of millions of years of evolutionary history. We start our lives inside our mother's wombs. There is not much to see inside that dark chamber.

Then we are born into a world chuck full of visual stimuli and sensation. Because of our genes, we are born with a desire to look around, to explore the world visually. We are born able to control our eye movements and not much else. Everywhere we look there is something else to see. This eye control allows the development of eye contact as the first channel of social communication.

As we look around at first our brains see two images, one from the right eye and the other from the left eye. Because of our genetic history, our brains recognize this pattern of stimuli. This triggers a rearrangement of our visual cortex until the microscopic little stripes with the same image from both the right and left eyes are lying next to each other. As we look around, both eyes can now focus on the same thing and form one image. This interplay between the brain's readiness and the stimulus from the world surrounding the baby is amazing, but it goes on.

About three months of age, we have started to develop head control. While lying down, we can turn our heads from side to side. This greatly expands our visual world. Now while looking straight-ahead we can take in much more of the surrounding visual world by turning our heads. Like a movie camera, we can pan. Using both eyes, this action brings in a mountain of 3-D visual information from our surroundings. Our genetic endowment allows us to recognize this new pattern of stimuli. It triggers another reorganization in our brain. This time the columns of neurons change. Now we can see stereoscopically. Our visual world is no longer flat.

This interplay between our surroundings and our genes goes on all throughout our life and is called memory and learning. This process never stops forming and reforming our brains changing who we are as our personal history unfolds. It is especially important during infancy and childhood when most of our development takes place. The learning of social communication and language is a product of this process. The interplay required for acquiring these skills has not been as well studied as 3-D vision. Nevertheless, it is hard to imagine how the underlying principles can be much different.

In the opinion of the author, it is time to stop trying to understand our brains by attributing so much to genetic factors and so much to environmental factors. That is like trying understanding what cloth is by pulling the threads apart. The real question is always how both factors weave together to explain human behavior and experience in the world we find ourselves living in.

By the way, once the infant has acquired depth perception, he is ready to start sharing visual experiences with his caregivers, the initiation of joint attention.

Brain- Capability, Behavior and Plasticity

The development of depth perception has been studied in great detail, and we can use it as a general model of brain capability and behavior. First, we are born with a range, or a spectrum, of abilities due to various genetic factors. There are a multitude of genes that can affect the brain, and it will take at least a century of diligent research to figure them all out.

Just the same I will make the hypothesis that any *brain function* that produces an observable behavior will have the following characteristics:

1) Genetic Potential: There will be a range of different inherent capabilities found in the general population to produce any given behavior. These differences are caused by genetic factors present at conception.

2) Readiness: The brain must be at a certain developmental point to acquire any behavior. Complex behaviors are built upon capabilities previously acquired.

3) Learning: The behavior will never emerge if the growing infant and child do not find enough of the right stimulation to induce its development. Learning will take place through observation, social imitation, and rewards/punishments coming from people in their surrounding social networks.

4) Critical Period and Brain Plasticity: There is often an optimum time for the brain to acquire a capability. Past this critical period, the brain can still change and learn the capability, but it is more difficult. It requires more motivation, attention and effort. The good news is that to a certain extent with practice, time, and effort it can be done. This ability to learn and acquire new abilities past the time of the critical period is called Brain Plasticity.

The model applies to practically any brain capability producing any behavior, ranging from the simple to the complex. It applies to the process of learning how to throw a ball, speak a language, dance, converse, or walk. Since we all have different genetic material, the anatomy and electro-biochemistry of each of our brains are all a little different. This will be discussed in more detail in the Chapter Five.

After conception, the development of our brains is shaped by our interactions with the world around us, our history. This begins in the womb while we are carried by our mothers. Inside the womb, we can hear the language and sounds of our mother's voice. We feel the motion as she walks around, and this motion lulls us to sleep as we comfort ourselves by sucking our fingers.

So even in the womb, there is self-involvement and social involvement. These forces are no doubt helping to shape our brains. But only at birth do we meet the world in full force. Our brains can only develop so much without stimuli from the outside world. These stimuli are needed to *induce* the development of our brains.

Our brains are prepared and ready to learn any number of capabilities from birth. But, like a handshake, we need to meet and react to the outside world in order to actually develop these potential capabilities. Our brains need to be customized to become a part of the world we are born into.

The ability for our brains to be customized during our very long childhoods while under the love and protection of our enduring social networks is the key to our species' spectacular evolutionary success, in my opinion.

Learning- Imitation and the Mirror Neuron System

As the infant meets the world during the first year of life need-states arise that can only be satisfied by learning new ways of action. Once he can make sense of the visual world about him, he can start to learn by observation and imitation how to do these things.

There is a special system in the brain called the *mirror neuron system* that is very involved with observation and imitation. It involves a special area of the brain. It reacts to the observation of the actions of other people. For instance there might be a neuron that responds to the observation of someone catching a ball. This neuron fires when this action is observed regardless of who is catching the ball or whether the catch takes place near or far. The observation of anyone catching a ball at any time will cause that neuron to respond.

That is amazing feat of brain organization. But then the mirror part comes in. Without actually moving a muscle, neurons that would be needed by us to physically imitate the catch fire off in turn, mirroring the catch in our own mind. This represents a mental imitation of the observed action. As these observations are repeated, and as the same group of neurons fire off repeatedly, some learning will take place.

My daughter goes to a gymnastic class. At each class, she seems to learn so much even though she only gets a few turns at any activity. I was puzzled by this until I realized she was learning by watching the other children take their turns as well, using her mirror neuron system.

Just as there are mirror neurons that mirror observed body movements, there are mirror neurons that mirror sensations and emotions. When we see someone being touched, we, in a sense, feel that touch as well. Likewise, when we see someone happy or any other emotion, our mirror neurons for that emotion will fire off. This is the core of empathy.

I remember in college we had an expression, a 'contact high', for the feeling you would get from being around friends who were feeling very good. Now I understand we had our mirror neuron system to thank for the fun. Likewise the pleasure of watching movies or other forms of entertainment must come in part through this brain function.

We do not have mirror neurons for objects. No matter how many smiles we paint on a ball we don't, as an adult, feel the ball is really happy. Likewise, as adults, we don't feel the doll's eyes are watching us. For a baby this can be a harder distinction. It is this confusion between objects, living beings and people that is at the heart of ASD.

ASD is essentially a condition where children's brains process people as if they were simply objects, as if they had no internal intentions and no emotions or feelings. Being more or less without social communication, children with ASD see themselves as objects in a world of objects.

After all, we have two-way communication only with living creatures and only one-way communication with objects. As babies are exposed to *objects that mimic living beings and people* more and more, ASD will become more common. This blurry line between objects and people in the nursery is a phenomenon of modern life.

For a time it was thought that a failure in the development of this mirror neuron system was the core defect in ASD. Children with ASD do have problems with imitation of people. With further research it was found that the mirror neuron system operates normally in children with ASD. They just do not seem to have the interest to imitate other people. fMRI brain imaging studies show their brains process social stimuli such as faces the way most of us process objects and things.

The ability to play at imitating how other people act or feel is an advanced social skill. Its development requires advanced social interactive skills that are acquired by children long after the first year of life. The initial failure, during the first year of life in children with ASD, to develop simple social communication skills, such as joint attention, precludes its subsequent development.

The capability to learn via observation and imitation can be astounding. There are people who can watch a complicated dance step and then turn around and perform it instantaneously. This kind of learning provides the **how** in learning. We learn **how** to throw a ball, speak a language, and so forth by observation and imitation of other people in our social networks who already have these skills. This kind of memory for motor skills is called *'procedural memory'*.

The learning process for these skills involves joint attention as well. We observe how other people in our social network respond to our motions and behaviors as we acquire these skills. In this form of joint attention, there are three elements: the subject, the trusted observer, and the event (which in this case is our execution of a given skill). We learn by interpreting the reactions of the observer, who acts like a coach for us. Their approval shapes our behavior. Without joint attention, this form of learning is impaired to varying degrees in people with ASD.

Learning- Attention

Attention is the key to learning. Without attention, nothing is learned. Attention is really a way of saying that the brain is in a state ready to learn, explore and react to the world around us.

Our eyes reflect our attention. What we look at reflects what our brains are thinking about. Our eyes constantly make tiny very rapid movements called *saccades*. These saccades give away our innermost thoughts. They show what in the world in front of us is attracting the attention of our brains.

The odd thing is we have no conscious awareness of these eye movements and likewise do not consciously see these movements in the eyes of the people around us. It almost seems like magic how our brains put together all this jumpy visual information coming from the eyes and transform it into a kind of three-dimensional movie for us; what we end up seeing.

As I am writing this, I can feel the breeze coming through the window, hear the computer's little fan, and feel the cushion in my chair. I am not paying attention to these sensations very much. I have a need-based state I am focused on. My need-based state is to share my thoughts with you by writing this book. As I write these words and express my thoughts to you, I get a little closer to my goal and it feels good. The elements of attention are alertness, a need-based state, and a goal that hopefully can be realized.

There is another aspect of attention; suppose I am sitting in my room by myself and I hear a creaking noise in the hallway outside my room. I will quickly forget my book and listen attentively to the noise. Could it be the footsteps of an unwelcome stranger?

Our brains pay attention to the unexpected. That is to say they are constantly making predictions of what is expected to happen next. I suppose humans are the only species making predictions about what will happen in ten years but that is another issue. It is the unexpected that grabs our attention. For the child with ASD who cannot read the intentions of other people, the behavior of other people is full of surprises often startling and disturbing, hence their love of routine.

The unexpected can easily arouse fear. Fear will direct attention very quickly. Hope and fear are basic emotions that serve to focus attention and learning. The typical child learns what is fearful and what is hopeful by observing the behavior of the people around them. In ASD, hope and fear are often set off by normal events triggering abnormal behavior in the child unexpectedly. These reactions can be quite disturbing to the social networks around a child with ASD.

Learning- The Scaffolding

Learning is acquired one step at time. Many times there is a sequence of skills or abilities that must be acquired in a certain order to develop a certain capability. Later in Chapter Six, I will discuss language acquisition in some detail, which provides a wonderful example of this principle.

Most capabilities can be broken down in to sub-capabilities. Only when all the sub-capabilities are functional can the capability be learned. A child cannot learn to write cursive lettering until he can hold a pencil, make a straight line, make a loop, and recognize letters. Education is very concerned with the sequence of lessons needed to learn a certain bit of knowledge. For instance, addition cannot be learned until integers are understood. If each step is important for learning the next step, then failure to learn the initial step will cause a cascade of failures as each step requires the successful completion or acquisition of the prior step.

Reciting a Saga from memory.

Learning- The Role of Social Networks

The social network in which we live plays a very important role in selecting which capabilities we will have the motivation and interest to develop. For instance, some of us have the innate ability to memorize entire sagas word for word. In preliterate societies this capability was highly valued.

These long and intricate stories helped bind the culture together. They were passed on from generation to generation by people who committed them to memory. We are not talking about simple children's stories. Some of them were more like soap operas with many characters and a very complicated plot. The saga could be so long it would take several nights to recite the entire story.

Imagine a world without books, radio, writing, or any way to record speech; almost all communication was two-way and face-to-face. My guess is ASD was very rare at that time. Humankind lived like that up until a few thousand years ago. How thrilling it must have been in those times to hear the old and treasured stories of your culture!

Today in India there are still a few men who can recite these amazing sagas and continue this oral tradition. Sadly, their sons do not have much interest in carrying on this tradition. It will soon be an amazing ability mankind will lose, not because humans have lost the inherent ability to perform this task, but because it is no longer valued in our social networks; it is not needed and will be soon forgotten.

Aside from personal survival there is no stronger motivation for humans than the hope and fear we find in being a part of our social networks. In fact, individual survival for most people is secondary to the well-being of their social groups. History is full of examples of people dying in order to defend these groups. We call such people heroes and admire their courage. We are loyal to the groups we belong to, be they our families, nations, religions, castes, political parties, or whatever.

In the course of human history, in order for a social network to survive, it had to be able to protect its members from other human social networks that would have gladly enslaved or exterminated them. The social networks that exist today in the world are the ones that have survived this competition for one reason or another.

It can be argued the two key functions for the survival of any social network are reproduction and defense. As an aside, is it fair to say females are somewhat genetically specialized for reproduction and males are specialized for defense? Do females' inherent interests in social matters enhance their ability to form the enduring relationships needed to protect and raise children? Do males' inherent interests in objects enhance their ability to handle weapons in warfare?

Hope and fear of future events drive the members of a social network to cooperate and to perform acts of self-sacrifice. Hope and fear also motivate and direct members of networks to learn the abilities expected of them. In the child with ASD, this fundamental motivation to meet the needs of the social network is blunted or absent. Instead, the child's motivation to learn is self-directed in a kind of social network with only one member: the child himself.

Behavior and the Brain Itself

What is going on in the brain to produce behavior? This is a very big question that is being intensely studied. However, one thing is clear: different parts of the brain have different roles. There are different anatomic locations for hearing, seeing, understanding language, forming thoughts into language, speaking, sleeping, emotions and so on.

Many years ago when I studied neuro-anatomy in medical school, the brain was more or less a mystery with white tracts going here and there and gray nuclei of uncertain purposes. To me it was best described as a confusing jumble of anatomy. Today, we currently have much better tools to study the brain. For instance, different fluorescein dyes can be used to study the biochemical pathways of individual neurons in different parts of the brain.

fMRI, a form of brain imaging, can measure the blood flow to a given area of the human brain down to a resolution of 3 mm. As an area in the brain becomes metabolically active, the blood flow increases. This can be seen on the fMRI and can demonstrate which areas of the brain are involved in a certain brain function.

Evoked action potential is another technique used to study the brain. It can measure the timing and strength of the brain's electrical activity. It helps us understand the timing and location of certain brain activities taking place near the outer surface of the brain.

These techniques and others have given us a real window into the anatomic functioning of the brain. The details of neuro-anatomy are beyond the scope of this book. I will only talk about the anatomy of brain in the most basic fashion.

It is no surprise there is a lot of sending of signals from one part of the brain to another before any behavior is produced. This intra-brain communication is needed to coordinate all our senses to produce a consistent picture of the world around us. A lot of this coordination happens in the cerebellum, an area of the brain that sits behind the cerebral cortex. The brain has to integrate all the senses and form a unified picture before deciding how to react next.

The parts of the brain that control memory, judgment, planning, need-based states, theory of mind, theory of culture, and even moral values all get involved in deciding what to do next. The frontal lobes of the cerebral cortex are involved in making these executive decisions. After that, the reaction needs to be coordinated and delivered through the nerves actually controlling the muscles and producing the behavior. Again the cerebellum is involved in coordination of body actions. Sometimes the reaction has to be virtually instantaneous and other times the brain will spend a lifetime cogitating over a given thought, producing no behavior at all.

But we do not react just to the stimuli the outside world presents to us. We also react to the stimuli our own bodies present to our brains. As a physician I spend a lot of my day interpreting stimuli such as pain or discomfort and hopefully fixing the underlying problem causing them. There is a third source of stimuli for the brain: the brain itself. These stimuli originate from some mental process in the brain producing a need-based state.

For instance, take hunger. The sensation of hunger creates a goal to find something that hopefully will satisfy that need-based state. In other words: *find food and eat*. You start looking for some tasty food and when you find some, you walk over to the food and start eating. The acts of looking, walking, and eating are all observable behaviors. The stimulus, hunger, comes from the brain. It is not visible to anyone else.

Eventually we get full and stop eating. Again that signal to change our behavior and to stop eating comes from our brain. It is true the feeling of hunger comes in part from a change in the body's internal chemical state, but it can also come from seeing, tasting, or smelling food, as well as the perception of the time of day and so on. The brain integrates these factors together before turning on the hunger need-based state.

In the same way, many factors besides the intake of food can cause hunger to go away. For instance, fear will take away hunger in an instant. These other factors are also mediated through brain activity. There is actually a satiety center with a specific physical location in the brain with this specialized function, making the feeling of hunger go away.

The brain can also be the source of its own stimuli without any connection to any input from the outside world or from within our bodies. Clearly, it can do this with or without producing any observable behavior. Using our brains, we can think, worry, plan, calculate, imagine, fantasize, and a thousand other things without any stimuli coming from inside or outside our bodies and without producing any movement. We may or may not be even aware of this activity going on in our brains. This brain activity is what I am calling *self-communication* or *self-involvement*.

You can imagine this kind of brain activity could sometimes form a loop where a series of thoughts, or a neural pathway, starts and returns to the same place again and again. Part of the loop could be some behavior, for instance, making a clicking noise with the mouth. If nothing breaks the repeating series of thoughts of a person caught in this loop, you might observe the repetitive behavior and/or the narrowly focused interests characteristic for a person with ASD.

Learning and ASD- Conclusion

Aside from fear, the most powerful motivator for normal people comes from the hope of obtaining pleasure. Pleasure often comes from the shared attention of the people we know and love in our social networks. This is supposed to begin with our first interactions with our first caregiver, who is almost always our mothers. This motivator starts a cascade of learning with the help and attention of our caregivers.

Using this motivator, the need for attention, we learn the skills and capabilities needed for effective social communication. This in time will lead to our integration into the networks within which we live. This learning comes through imitation and endless episodes of joint attention with the trusted people in our social networks.

Self-involvement and self-stimulation can also be pleasurable, especially for boys. Any experience that rewards self-involvement, especially during the first year of life, can drive these children along the spectrum away from social communication and towards excessive enjoyment of self-involvement.

Excessive self-involvement starts a cascade of idiosyncratic learning experiences which move the child away from social integration into his family. Experiences that reward self-involvement, such as watching television and other forms of one-way communication, play a major role as the environmental cause of ASD.

The behaviors we observe in children with ASD arise from an imbalance between too little of the brain function I am calling *social communication* and too much of the brain function I am calling *self-involvement*.

During the first year of life, millions of neurons die, in order to customize our brains to fit our needs. Usage helps decide which neurons will be needed and which won't. It has been recently found that children with ASD have an excess of neurons in the areas in the brain specialized to serve social communication, the so-called 'social brain'. This, I suppose, means that the normal death of neurons that occurs during the first year of life in these areas of the brain is not happening. Perhaps lack of usage of the social brain in children with ASD is the cause of this failure of the normal neural pruning process.

Over a lifetime our brains are formed and re-formed by our interaction with the world around us. Who we are today is a reflection of our genetic heritage and our personal history and its effect on our brain. Memories are formed, some transient and others enduring. Skills are acquired and lost. And throughout it all our social networks form the backdrop of our life, the stage upon which our life is played.

The next section of this book goes on to investigate the actual causes of ASD. It is known ASD is largely a male problem: there are four times as many boys than girls with ASD. When you look at high-functioning people with the Asperger's form of ASD the ratio is said to be seventeen boys to one girl. This striking difference begs an explanation. The next chapter discusses gender and what it tells us about the nature and causes of ASD.

About Otto – Four
Rosangela's Stories- One

In Rosangela's words…

Once in a shopping mall they had an attraction. The attraction consisted in making a kid to have a sensation of walking on top of the water. The child would get inside an inflatable ball. The child was put inside the ball while it was still deflated. The ball was then sealed and inflated with air. Then the ball was thrown inside a very shallow swimming pool. As the child would walk inside the ball he would have the impression of walking on top of the water.

Otto saw the children having fun with it and wanted to participate of the activity, too. He got inside the ball, but when the ball started to be inflated he got desperate (maybe because of the loud noise or maybe because of being in a closed place or maybe both). I soon noticed that he was not doing well so I requested he be removed from the ball.

When Otto got out of the ball Marcio [his father] asked him why he could not do it and to look around all the other kids having fun with it. As a reply Otto said, "Ok, Dad I will try it again!" For the second time he got inside of the ball and as soon as the noise from the pump started, he began to cry.

I asked for the worker to stop the procedure and to remove Otto from there. As soon as Otto got out of the bubble he ran desperately through the mall. We chased him everywhere. Marcio was deeply embarrassed and repeated, "Let's go home, let's go home!" Otto then, stopped, lay down, and kept repeating, "I don't want to go home, it is ok I will get into the ball…"

Marcio wanted go home because he could not handle Otto's behavior in front of the public. In Otto's mind his father wanted to leave because he had failed in his attempts to participate in the ball activity.

So I did the following: I put Erik [his brother] in Marcio's lap and asked him to go for a walk with him on the next floor up. I laid down on the floor with Otto and talked to him. I explained to him the reason that his father wanted to leave was not his failure in participating in the activity. The activity was not important for us.

What his father did not want was his running around the mall without waiting for us. When the explanation was clear in Otto's mind, we got up and met Marcio and Erik and kept our shopping routine.

- Rosangela Eicher

Author's Comments

Otto sees the other children having fun and wants to join. He struggles to calm his idiosyncratic reaction to his enclosure in the ball and the loud noise and fails. Fear wins. The surrounding social network fails to reassure his native reactions.

After leaving the ball, the fear has no doubt stirred up a powerful fight or flight reaction. He chooses to run, oblivious to the cultural norms and subsequent embarrassment and shame felt by his family.

Chapter Four
Gender

Why are boys so much more susceptible to ASD? What is going on in their brains that makes them so vulnerable to this condition? We know boys and girls have bodies that are different. Later after puberty, their bodies will become even more different. But what about their minds? Cultural influences aside, is there a real difference between a girl's mind and brain from a boy's? If so, when does this start and how does this difference impact their social development?

In this chapter, I will talk about these differences and how they help us understand how ASD develops. Again, we will be looking at how a genetic factor like gender interacts with the surrounding environment to change and shape the minds and brains of our children.

Introduction to Gender and ASD

Gender, whether a child is male or female, is genetic. The presence of one X and one Y chromosome are found in a normal male whiles two X chromosomes are the rule in a normal female. There are variations on these combinations, but they are beyond the scope of this book. Nevertheless gender is clearly genetic.

Gender has a large role in the causation of ASD. There is a remarkable difference between boys and girls in the incidence of ASD. The ratio is usually quoted as 4 males to 1 female. As the level of functioning and cognitive ability increases, the ratio of males to females increases. The ratio of males to females with Asperger's, a high functioning form of ASD, is said to be an incredible seventeen males for each female. However, when the IQ of a child is less than 50, which is a very low level of cognition, the ratio of males to female is almost equal.

Whatever is causing this tilted sex ratio is more than just the difference between how boys and girls are raised, but reflects a genuine innate genetic difference between human males and females. When I was young I could have easily given you a long list of how females and males differed from each other. As expectations in our culture have changed the differences between the sexes have narrowed down considerably. ASD is one area where the difference remains.

How can gender affect the development of our brains? Without getting too complicated, there are two general ways this can happen. The first is from the genes located on the sex chromosomes, usually the X chromosome. The X chromosome is much, much bigger than the Y chromosome, and has many more genes. When something goes wrong with one of the many genes on the single X chromosome in a male, the problem will be expressed. Females have two copies of the X chromosome which means one copy can effectively act as a backup. In females, both X chromosomes need to be faulty for a problem to be expressed.

Could the problem causing ASD be on the X chromosome? This has been studied extensively and the quick answer is by and large no, with the exception of the Fragile X syndrome. We will look more at the genetic factors that can cause ASD including the Fragile X syndrome in the next chapter.

There is another way gender can affect our brains. The two genders produce different sex hormones. These hormones enter the blood stream and can produce widespread effects in our bodies and our brains. These effects cause the male and female developmental paths to diverge.

In human males there are two surges of testosterone, the male hormone, before puberty. The first surge starts during gestation between the fourth and sixth weeks of pregnancy and lasts for a few months. This first surge is responsible for the difference between male and female anatomy. The second surge comes at the time of birth. The testosterone levels rise in males for a few months and then return to a low level until puberty. In other mammals this surge causes differences to develop in the behavior of the sexes. This surge is the one that causes ASD in males according to Simon Baron-Cohen in his theory called *The Extreme Male Brain Theory of Autism*.

Much of the remaining material in this chapter comes from the work of Simon Baron-Cohen. He has investigated this area and written about it extensively. His theory states there are two types of brains: male and female. The differences in the brains are caused by the second surge of testosterone in the male. This surge, according to Baron-Cohen, makes the male brain more systemizing while leaving the female brain in a more empathetic state.

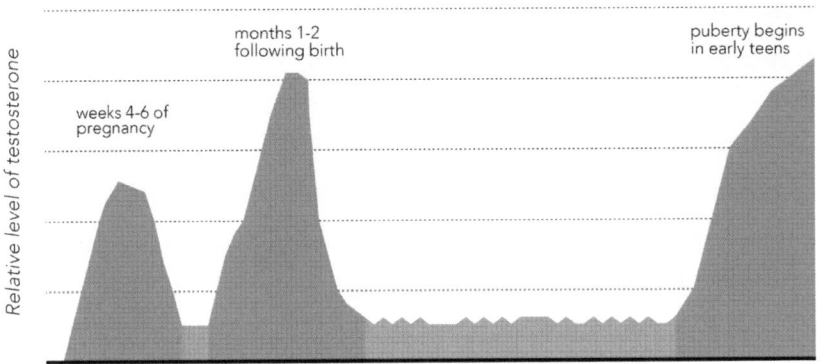

The Female Brain- Empathy

Baron-Cohen characterizes the female brain as being more empathetic. By empathy, he is referring to the ability to identify the emotional states of other people and form an appropriate reaction to another person's emotions, thoughts and feelings. This leads to a female being more likely to feel another person's pain. As evidence he cites studies that have shown girls are less likely to engage in roughhouse play compared to boys. He also cites studies showing grown women are less likely to be aggressive, sociopathic, or to become murderers. He attributes all these findings to females having higher inherent levels of empathy as compared to males.

There is a third surge of testosterone at the time of puberty. This surge initiates all the sexual changes found during adolescence. Testosterone by itself is known to cause aggressive behavior. So the difference between adult males and females in the area of aggressiveness may be due to the hormonal differences that arise during puberty, and not necessarily to the changes that occurred in the male brain at the time of birth during the second testosterone surge.

The Female Brain- Social Communication

There are other traits Baron-Cohen includes in his discussion of the female brain. These traits can be grouped together as being connected to social communication, which fits right in with the overall theme of this book. These are traits reflecting females' inherent superiority in the area of social communication. In general females derive more pleasure from and have more ability in social interactions than males. Furthermore, even an ordinary conservation is no simple thing.

Imagine for a moment all the brain functions needed to conduct a two-way face-to-face conversation. There is the brain function of observing and attending to all the details of facial expression, especially the eyes. Eye movements give away our inner thoughts but they are too fast to be understood by our conscious brains. Nevertheless poker players go to great lengths to hide these eye movements from the other players.

There is likewise a brain function for observing *body language*. After making these observations, another brain function is needed to take all this sensory information and integrate it together to form a unified picture. While all this is going on, still another part of the brain is listening and paying attention to what is being said.

Language, of course, is very important in conversation. Understanding spoken language is another brain function, and an amazingly complicated one at that. To get to the meaning of what is being said the brain needs to know the meanings of words, the grammar, the syntax and so on. Then it is not only the choice of words that matters, it is also how the words are spoken, the prosody of the language.

The rhythm, the intonation and the volume of speech all have meaning. The meaning of a spoken language, depending on how the words are spoken, can easily be the exact opposite of what the words literally mean. The meaning can also be purposely ambiguous or even humorous. A particular brain function has to process all this information to make sense of the spoken words. And so it goes on. Then the brain integrates all this information and infers what the other person is thinking or feeling. This brain function is called *theory of mind* as discussed in Chapter One.

If this conversation is with someone who is in one of our social networks, someone with whom we have an ongoing relationship, then another brain function is needed to integrate this interaction with our memories about prior experiences with this person. This picture needs to be recalled from some other part of our brain. Is it getting complicated? This is just the start of the process, the receptive part.

There is another series of brain functions required for expression, which are equally, if not more, complicated. They involve judgments, plans, awareness of our surroundings and our bodies, organizing our next action and so on.

Somewhere in the midst of all these brain functions, another part of the brain is providing attention and emotional interest, including fear and hope, while imagining the anticipated future both near and far. These feelings are driving the conversation forward.

Again, if this is an ongoing relationship, then the brain needs to integrate this interaction into the *theory of culture*. By this, I mean the brain has to integrate this interaction into the context of the common beliefs and ideas of the cultures of whatever social networks the people in the conversation share.

Weaving throughout all this is an appreciation of the other person's point of view, which includes an idea of how they are viewing us and vica versa.

My goodness, this process is extremely complicated. But it happens all day long very rapidly in real time, no replay or rehearsal allowed, virtually every day of our lives, and really provides the meaning to our existence.

The point is that females, measured as a group, are better at these brain functions insofar as they can be measured. The difference is already manifested in infants. From the start, baby girls have more interest in and take more pleasure from social communication. Female newborns look at faces and at peoples' eyes longer and more frequently than boys. Newborn girls prefer looking at faces as compared to a mobile, while for boys it is the opposite. Girls start pointing earlier than boys as a means of sharing joint attention.

Girls also show joint attention before boys, which is critical for the development of social communication. Furthermore, girls understand language before boys and also begin speaking earlier. At sixteen months they can typically speak 100 words, while a boy normally speaks only 30 words. In short, girls have more interest and abilities in social communication than boys. This difference shows up during the first and second years of life, during the critical period for acquiring social communication. Newborn girls are primed to join and be a part of the social network of their family.

As baby girls grow up, this interest and aptitude for social interaction continues. They like to talk and share in conversations. They also like talking about their emotions. They take the other person's perspective in to account in conversations and are better at language skills. I agree with Baron-Cohen. Female minds are inherently better than male minds in social communication. This difference starts from birth. They develop a better understanding of what makes *people* tick and a better grasp of other people's points of view. That is a good part of the reason why so many fewer girls have ASD than boys.

The Male Brain- The Systemizer

If girls are so good at social communication, what are boys good at? Baron-Cohen, in his extreme male brain theory of autism, would say boys are good at *systemising*. By systemising, he means understanding the behavior of non-living objects and things that follow the laws of physics or other principles. They develop a better understanding of what make *things* tick.

I agree. I think boys, when compared to girls, enjoy experiences with things and objects more; as infants they like to watch things move, fall, roll and so forth. While the baby girl is looking at the face, the baby boy is looking at the mobile move. Studies show boys are better at figuring out what happens to a rolling ball than girls. They pay less attention to people and more attention to objects.

This kind of mental activity is not social communication. It can be looked as a form of one-way communication from the outside world to the boy's inner world. There is no back and forth conversation between an object and the infant. The pleasure for the boy, which is not necessarily shared with anyone, comes from satisfying an inherent interest in the physical world and comes entirely from within the baby boy.

If one could imagine the stream of consciousness in a baby boy, it might go something like this: "Oh boy, look at the ball rolling and now stopping. Wow!" This is self-communication. If anything, another person interfering with this observation of the physical world might be a bother, a distraction. It would disturb the peace and pleasure derived from the self-involvement and the contemplation of the real world.

A neurotypical boy might want to share this experience with his caregiver and add a secondary level of pleasure via social communication, but the underlying interest and pleasure in the boy's interaction with the object does not require social contact or joint attention.

Now, how interesting can non-living things be for an infant? During all of human history before the last 50 years, I would have said: not very. It is true a rattle can be fascinating for a baby, but it is nothing compared to the toys, video devices and televisions of today. But that is a story for later in the book.

So boys are fascinated by the objects whose movements follow principles described by physics. In contrast, the girls like social beings whose actions are determined by internal intentions. To truly understand how the world around us operates we need to be able to understand both. There is a fascinating tension between the two points of view that is beyond the scope of this book.

Boys may grow up to be better systemizers than girls. I will not venture to guess how much of this is a function of our culture and how much is genetic. Nor will I speculate on how much this interest in objects and things lays the groundwork to help solve problems systematically. However, there is a difference in the male brain that pertains directly to the cause of ASD. It is this inherent fascination in the behavior of objects in the physical world which leads directly to self-involvement and self-communication. This is another part of the reason why so many more boys have ASD than girls.

What do these differences tell us about the genders? Are they really so different? As a whole, I think the normal male and female brains are much more similar than they are different. However, ASD highlights one real difference: girls are social communicators and boys are self-communicators. Girls are more interested in people and boys are more interested in objects.

For instance, I remember spending hours thinking about the problem of how to build a three wheeled car when I was in middle school. I would run over various designs in my mind, picturing how they would steer or park, or how they would react in an accident. These details always seemed to me much more important than whatever the teacher was talking about. And who liked who in the class was a question that struck me as having little weight or importance.

But I do not think that more of one faculty always means less of the other. We should all strive to have our children be good at both brain functions; let them all be little Benjamin Franklins.

Benjamin Franklin Discovers the Nature of Lightning

Benjamin Franklin at the Constitutional Congress

You will find many girls who are very good at self-communication and many boys who are very good at social communication. But we cannot ignore the differences, either. We have to assume boys are more vulnerable to influences that interfere with the learning of social communication.

These differences between boys and girls are clearly genetic, as gender is determined by the sex chromosomes. These differences may be mediated by the testosterone surge that occurs in boys about the time of birth.

The girls seem to have more of the need-state for the attention of the people around them, the boys less. This sets the stage for a real vulnerability in the boys. The theme of this book is about how the interplay between this genetic vulnerability and all the one-way communication surrounding infants today leads to ASD.

Overall, I think Baron-Cohen is correct in his theory about autism. The theory explains why for every girl with ASD there are four boys. This is a profound genetic contribution to the cause of ASD. However, there are lots of other genetic factors involved in the causation of this condition. They will be discussed in the next chapter.

About Otto – Five
Rosangela's Stories- Two

In the first consultation with the neurologist, he asked for a MRI. Otto was sedated for the test. My mother and I took Otto to do the test. After the test was done, Otto had difficulties in wakening up. We waited for about 20 minutes when the nurse asked me to wake him up.

I asked my mother to talk to the nurse to wait while I would grab a hot chocolate and wake him up as in our daily morning routine at home. I went to the end of the hall where the beverage machine was located and while the machine was still filling the cup I heard Otto screaming.

I left everything and ran towards his room. I arrived at the room and found Otto underneath the bed, screaming and punching everything and everybody, including himself. He was hurting himself and acting as a cornered wild animal. His little arm had blood everywhere. When I tried to approach him he ran from me. He would throw himself on the wall; he wanted to throw everything on the floor. He wanted to break everything in front of him.

I was crying my eyes out and asked my mother what had happened. She said that Otto woke up when the nurse tried to remove the tape from the IV site. Otto pulled out the IV himself, jumped from the bed and acted crazy like that.

Otto was screaming and he was very angry. He would not allow anyone to approach him. Doctors and nurses came to try to help but he would punch and kick everybody. This situation took more than one hour. I could not handle it anymore and grabbed Otto by force and went to the car.

Inside of the car I locked him in the child seat but he got loose and wanted throw himself through the window. I tried to calm him down for a long time. I tried to drive but he would throw himself on top of the steering wheel and I could not drive. My mother could not help or hold him.

I took him out of the car for a walk but he would not stop screaming and wanted to run like a mad man and did not want me to follow him. I did not have a choice. I put him back inside of the car and we waited until he calmed down. After a long wait he lay down on the back seat and started crying and sobbing he said: "Mom, I am so sorry!" Then he cried himself to sleep.

- Rosangela Eichler

Chapter Five
Genetics

What other evidence points to genetic influences for ASD aside from gender? How does the study of twins with ASD help answer this question? Are there genetic influences on social communication? The evidence I will discuss in this chapter is quite strong and multifaceted. But overall, the genetic influence is less than many investigators believe.

Our Bodies Built for Receptive Communication

To begin with, though it seems obvious to state, we are born with a body made for social communication. Our eyes and our brain, working together, see and interpret facial expressions and body language. No matter where you go in the world, facial expressions are a universal language understood by all humans. Humans always have a spoken language, too. Our ears and our brain's auditory system are built to hear and process speech. Our bodies also respond to the basic and powerful language of touch. All our senses are used for social communication.

Though most people immediately think of language when they think of social communication, smell is also a fascinating area in which to study interpersonal communication. We use smell to communicate and coordinate activities without any conscious awareness or control. It has been known for some time women subconsciously communicate by smell: when they live or work in the same place, the time of their periods tends to synchronize. This effect is mediated through smell.

Likewise, a recent study has shown men can detect an ovulating woman by smell. Ovulation is the time of the month a woman is most likely to get pregnant. Neither women nor men are consciously aware when a woman is ovulating. However, men find an ovulating woman inexplicably more attractive. This amazing feat of social communication is again mediated through smell. Some of what we call 'getting a feeling' about another person may actually be mediated by smell.

My dog, whose sense of smell is light years beyond mine, seems to understand me at times better than I understand myself. He can detect odors on me I cannot even imagine. My dog and I have different preferred channels of social communication. His favorite is smell, while mine is spoken language. But we both like body language, touch, and facial expressions. Dogs are one of the few species actually comfortable with eye to eye contact with humans. This is sufficient for the good relationship we have.

Our bodies are built to sense the outside world, including forms of communication originating from other people. We need and use our senses for a multitude of other things as well. They allow us to navigate through space and time. They are our **here and now**. But they are all also receptive organs for communication.

Our Bodies Built for Expressive Communication

Two Italian men gesticulating

What about the other side, the expressive side? Unless we are looking in a mirror, we are quite unaware of our own facial expressions, while the people around us can read this channel of communication quite clearly.

Of course, we use body language and touch to express ourselves to other people. In this country, you can forget how rich this form of communication can be; touching is usually limited to handshakes and body language is very subdued. Going to Italy, where most people gesticulate extensively while speaking, makes you aware of the many delightful messages that humans are capable of expressing with the movements of their bodies.

Monks sworn to silence using sign language

Sign language, which freed the deaf from social isolation, is a complete language in and of itself. Most people communicate vocally using our larynges (the voice box) to speak, sing, shout, or scream. The larynx is an excellent and extraordinary producer of sound.

However, its basic purpose is not related to speech. Air, carrying oxygen, and food, carrying nutrition, must both pass through the mouth. Air goes to our lungs, and food must be transported into the stomach. The larynx directs the traffic. The lungs do not do well inhaling food, water, or, worse yet, stomach contents, so the larynx has the vital job of protecting our airways. The other function of the larynx is to make sounds. Has the anatomy of the larynx evolved so humans can vocalize language?

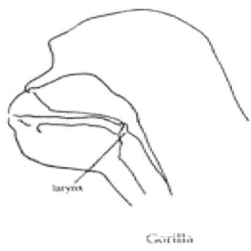
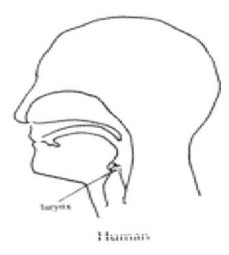

There is a difference found in the human larynx very few other animals have: it is called a *descended larynx*. This means the larynx sits lower in the neck than the usual position in other animals. For many years, this was thought to be unique to humans, but it is found in a few other species such as whales and red deer. In

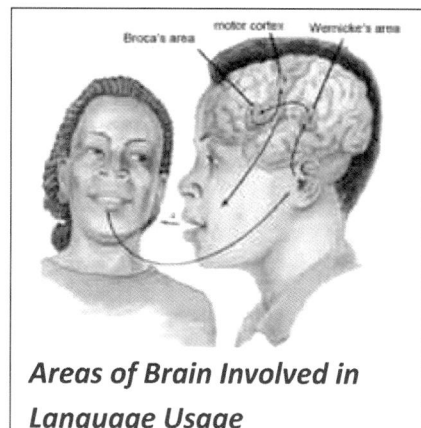

Areas of Brain Involved in Language Usage

humans, it enables the production of some important vowel sounds found in all languages.

However, the real difference in expressive communication separating humans from all other species is found, not surprisingly, in the brain. The brain is specialized in humans for language and social communication. There are special areas in the brain, which function together to make it possible for us to understand and express language. They have specific names such as Broca's and Wernicke's areas.

Broca's area is close to the area in the brain controlling the larynx. Damage to Broca's area will prevent a person, who is fully aware of what he wants to say, from being able to properly express himself. At the same time, this person usually, but not always, understands language perfectly. It is a complex area of study in and of itself, but for our purposes, let us say, this anatomic area of the brain has evolved to produce speech.

Wernicke's area is similarly adapted for language, but largely for receptive language. It is close to the brain's auditory area. People with damage to Wernicke's area have difficulty comprehending language, while speaking fluently. These same two areas in the brains of other primates are involved with the production of utterances and body language and its comprehension, so these human capabilities did not arrive without some evolutionary precedent. But in humans, they are specially adapted to meet the needs of human communication.

In other words, the process of human evolution has adapted these previously existing organs, the brain and larynx, to give them new and wonderful abilities. The ability to talk, sing, scream, or whisper comes from the structure of our human larynx and its coordination with our human brain. The fundamental purpose of these capabilities is social communication.

There is another characteristic of the human body which helps shape our ability to communicate socially: the appearance of our eyes. Our eyes are formed to emphasize the contrast between the white of the sclera and the color of our iris. Compare the chimpanzee eyes and the human eyes in the below image. No other animal has this contrast as strong as humans.

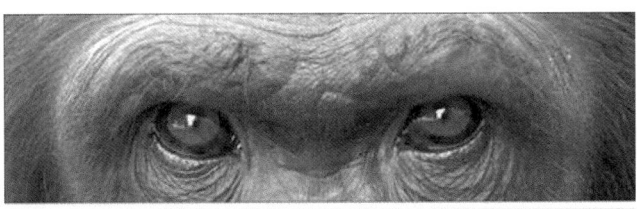
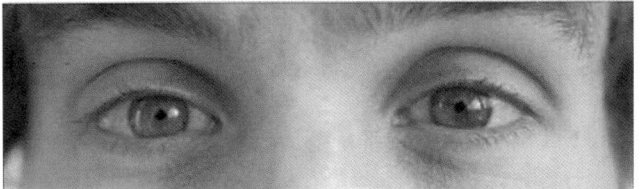

Why is that? Joint attention requires people to be able to follow the gaze direction of the other person. Having a high contrast between the white and colored parts of our eyes enables us to see where other people's eyes are pointed. This makes it easier to see what other people are looking at and to share that experience with them. This, in turn, makes joint attention possible, and joint attention is critical in the normal development of social communication. So even the coloration of our eyes reflects how our bodies have evolved to aid socialization. Furthermore, it is known our brain is fully capable of calculating the positions of our eyes and other peoples' eyes around us.

The point is our bodies demonstrate we are genetically endowed with a rich tool box to communicate with each other. Our genes are a product of the evolution of our species. Considering our ancestral species, we have been living together in groups for millions of years. Our bodies and our genes are the proof.

We are created with the potential to talk, listen, smile, touch, feel, and interpret the facial expressions of and let us not leave out smell the people around us. Only face-to-face communication allows us to use all of our senses to communicate. It is for this reason that people travel halfway around the world for business and pleasure: to meet other people face-to-face.

The Study of Twins with Autism

At the start of the book, I wrote about how in academic circles; the cause of ASD is thought to be 90% genetic. Why would be this so? Academics lead the great scientific enterprise of our time, specializing in the production and evaluation of evidence. While not always right and subject to human passions and whims, I think we all look to academia for answers to the tough problems we face as a culture.

Then why do so many academics think ASD is almost a purely genetic disorder? Where is the evidence supporting this point of view? The strongest evidence largely comes from the studies of twins who have or do not have ASD. I am going oppose the usual academic interpretation of these studies. I know opposing academia is a form of modern day heresy but here I go. I better have some good reasons for this heresy, reasons that everyone can understand.

I am going to try to explain these studies of twins in ASD as simply as I can. I hope to demonstrate how the interpretation of these studies has misled academics into more or less ignoring the importance of environmental factors in the cause of ASD.

Starting from basics, genes are the pieces of DNA that carry all the instructions livings things inherit from their parents. They are your recipe. They represent millions of years of evolutionary history. Traits are the things about you an investigator can see or test for. Are you tall or short? Are you good with numbers? Do you have ASD or not? Do you have blue eyes? These are some of the traits you carry.

Twin studies avoid the difficulty of isolating the contribution that *each individual gene* makes for any particular trait. They can answer the question: is a trait genetic or environmental? But twin studies cannot say whether this gene or that one is involved in producing any certain trait. For that matter, if a trait is shown to be largely genetic by twin studies it could come from one gene, several genes, or a combination of many different genes, each gene making a small contribution.

These studies allow investigators to look at the expression of the *sum total of all the genetic material* in a given person. Twins studies are an excellent way of teasing out the relative contribution of genetic versus environmental factors for any trait. If the twin studies do not show a significant genetic contribution then there is no point in looking for the individual or combination of genes responsible for that trait because the trait is environmental not genetic.

The trait we will be looking at is ASD. Twins studies on autism are very convincing for some genetic contribution to ASD although they are a bit confusing. I will try to make them easily understandable.

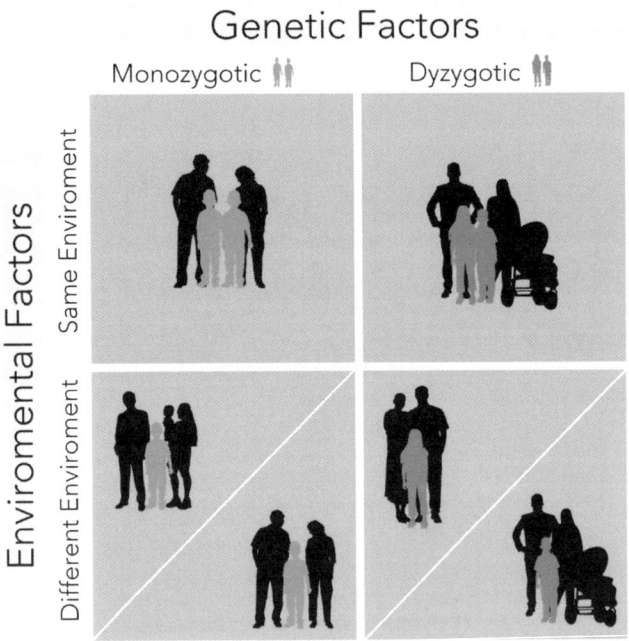

There are basically four kinds of twins: two genetic types and two environmental types. The genetic types are identical (monozygotic or MZ) twins, who have the identical starting genetic material, and fraternal (dizygotic or DZ) twins, who share the same amount of genetic material as any other two brothers or sisters would. The environmental types are twins who were raised together in the same family social network, presumably sharing many of the same experiences in childhood, and twins who were raised in separate families or cultures and whose personal histories are quite different.

Monozygotic and Dizygotic Twins

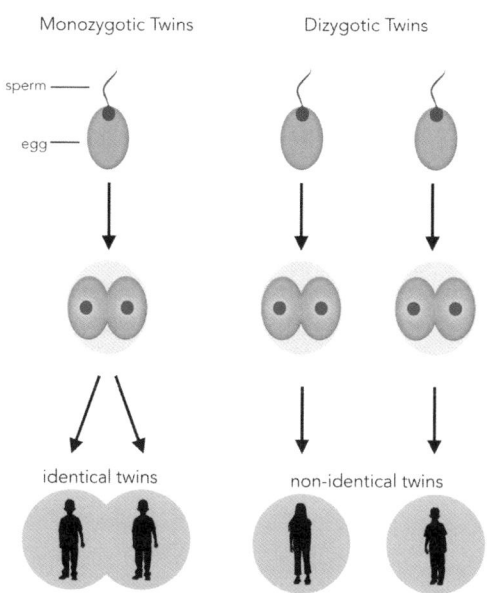

Identical twins are called monozygotic, or MZ, twins since they come from the same fertilized ovum, or egg. Fraternal twins are called dizygotic, or DZ, twins since they come from separate fertilized eggs. A *Trait* again is the name of any characteristic being looked at in a certain study.

A study may look at height, hair color, spoken language or anything else that can measured or observed by the investigator. Since hair color is determined by genes, you would expect two identical twins (MZ) to have exactly the same hair color, no matter what family they were raised in.

The language a child learns is determined by the family they live with. So if identical (MZ) twins are raised in different families each speaking a different language, you would expect each child would speak the respective language of their family. So, we would say the actual language spoken by a child is determined by non-genetic factors, namely by the language the child was exposed to during the critical period for language learning. The more a trait is found in both MZ twins regardless whether they were raised in different families and cultures, the more likely it is to be a genetic factor.

In the real world, very few twins are separated at birth, so we have too few twins like that to make this kind of study. So instead of making that comparison, studies usually compare the frequency of a trait in MZ twins versus DZ twins. Both twins in these studies live together in the same family and culture and share much of the same experiences.

If a given trait is shared more often in <u>both</u> MZ twins compared to <u>both</u> DZ twins, then that is strong evidence the trait is caused by a genetic factor. In general, you would expect the frequency of sharing a given genetic trait in DZ twins to be the same as any another sibling (brother or sister). This is because the DZ twins share the same amount of genetic materials as any other sibling. So if one DZ twin has blue eyes, what are the chances the second DZ twin will have blue eyes? The chances are the same as any other sibling with the same biological mother and father.

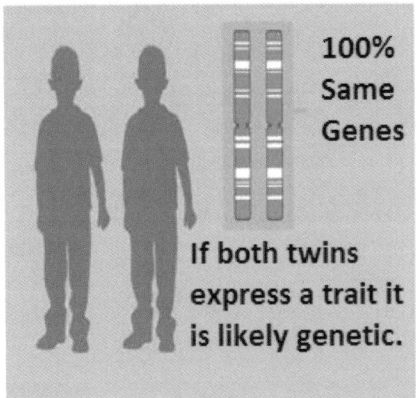
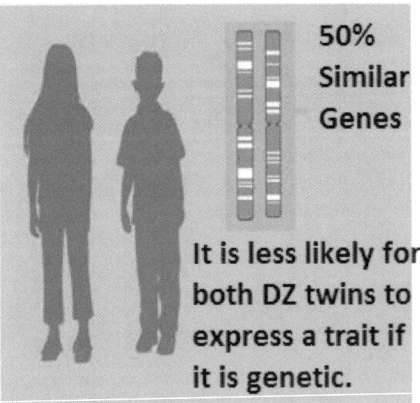

Simply put, the study of twins goes like this: first the investigator measures the frequency both twins have a given trait. That measurement is called *concordance*. If, for instance, you measure hair color in a group of twins and in 70% of the time both twins have the same hair color, then you would say 70% of these twins were concordant in hair color. A big difference in concordance between MZ and DZ twins points to a genetic cause, while no difference points to an environmental cause. By measuring the difference in concordance between DZ twins and siblings in the general population, you will get an estimate of the effect that being raised with another twin has on the trait.

Studies Comparing MZ and DZ Twins with ASD

With that very brief discussion of the genetics of twins, let us look at ASD. When autism was first described, it was thought to be caused by what was called the *ice box mother*. In other words, it was thought to be caused by a problem in the maternal-child relationship, an environmental factor. The mothers were to blame. There were some small, inconclusive twin studies at that time which did not refute this hypothesis.

Then in 1977, a study was done on 21 twin pairs, of which 11 of the twin pairs were MZ and 10 were DZ. The study found a very big difference in the concordance rate between MZ twins and DZ twins. In thirty-six percent of MZ twins both twins had autism while **zero** percent of the DZ twins were concordant for autism.

This was very strong evidence for a major contribution of genetic factors in this condition. The study prompted everyone to start looking for genetic factors and the 'ice box mother' was fortunately quickly forgotten. This study included only twins strictly with autism, not milder cases with Asperger's or Pervasive Development Disorder that today would be grouped with ASD.

Since then, this kind of study comparing MZ and DZ twins has been repeated over and over again. These studies are not easy to do well. One problem is if you take two unusual conditions, such as twinning and autism, the number of children affected by both conditions at the same time is very small. The more children in a study the stronger the conclusions become. It is quite difficult to put together a good sized sample of children who are both autistic and twins.

Furthermore, diagnosing a child with ASD is not always straightforward. These studies all deal with children with that diagnosis. You could say the trait of ASD carries many sub-traits; how it is all put together to diagnose the child with this condition varies from one clinician to another.

Even the differentiation of MZ twins from DZ twins is not always as easy as you might imagine. These are important methodological problems for the investigator. Nevertheless, the studies have been done. Those studies have shown a big difference in the rates of concordance between MZ and DZ twins, pointing to a large genetic contribution in the causation of ASD.

Over time, the studies have broadened to look at the entire ASD spectrum and at younger and younger age groups. One recent such study looked at the entire ASD spectrum included twins found in a voluntary online ASD database. The study showed a difference in the concordance rates of 88% in MZ twins and 31% in DZ twins. A second study, based on the entire population of twins in Sweden, showed a concordance rate for ASD of 39% in MZ twins and 15% in DZ twins.

In general, the difference in the rates of concordance between MZ and DZ twins in these studies varied between 20% and 40% percent, with the lower differences being found in more recent studies using the entire spectrum of ASD. All in all, these studies are the strongest evidence for a genetic cause of ASD.

Studies Comparing MZ and DZ Twins with Sub-Traits of ASD

All the previously mentioned studies looked at ASD as one solitary trait. What if we break ASD apart and look at the individual sub-traits or criteria that go into making the diagnoses of ASD? Are these sub-traits inherited? How can we examine that?

Well, we have various tests for autism, from the Childhood Autism Spectrum Test to the Autism-spectrum Quotient and other similar tests. These tests ask questions about the different criteria used to diagnose ASD.

They may ask about different behaviors reflecting self-involvement such as focused interests, repetitive body movement, or overreactions to sensory stimuli. Likewise they may ask questions about impaired social communication such avoidance of eye contact, inability to understand body language, and impairment of speech. Each of these questions reflects a sub-trait found in children with ASD.

The parent, clinician, or researcher-observer answers the questions in the questionnaire about the child and a score is calculated. The more sub-traits of ASD a child has and the higher the score is on the test, the more likely the child is to actually have ASD.

Now an investigator can have a group of twins complete the test and compare the results between MZ and DZ twins. None of the twins has to actually have ASD for this kind of study, so the problem of finding adequate subjects is greatly reduced. As a result, these studies have much greater numbers of subjects. Instead of needing to make a full diagnostic evaluation on each subject, just a little questionnaire is needed. Many studies like this have been done, and what do we find?

First, we find the sub-traits of ASD are widely distributed in the population. There is no clear line separating children with ASD from other children. These studies are why ASD has the word 'spectrum' in the middle. There is a wide distribution of these traits of ASD throughout the general public in the cultures where it has been studied.

At first, the studies were done in older children and adults. They were older than 5 years old in these initial studies. The peak period to find children with ASD is around the age of seven, so this is a good time to detect the sub-traits of ASD. One typical study from 2005 looked at children between the ages 5 and 17 in Wales and northern England. The concordance between MZ twins was 73% and DZ twins was 38%. Another study in 2000 from Missouri in the same age group showed concordance between MZ male twins at 73% and DZ male twins at 37%.

ASD does not suddenly start at the age of five years. As the earlier findings and sub-traits of ASD were better described, tools for evaluating these sub-traits in younger children were developed. So studies were done with younger children.

One study out of Boston in 2009 reported concordance rates between male MZ twins at 58% and DZ twins at 38%. Another study in 2010 from Wisconsin showed rates of concordance in male MZ twins at 62% and DZ twins at 25%. The difference in concordance rates in the two groups was 37%. Both studies involved young children between 2 and 3 years old. These studies all taken together support a strong genetic influence for ASD. The studies also demonstrate many normal children also have some sub-traits of ASD.

Social Communication and Twins- A Special Case

MZ twins at birth

In all these studies, problems with social communication are counted as important traits; ones needed to diagnose ASD. However, none of the studies have looked at whether changes in the social communication environment of an infant could be a **cause** of ASD. This is the premise of the Integrated Theory of Autism, as stated by the author of this book.

What if being raised as a twin, and especially being an identical twin, is a risk factor in and of itself for ASD? If that is so, then these twin studies would overstated the genetic contribution to ASD.

Twins are a special instance of social communication. Since twins are usually raised together and are in each other's company from the time of conception, they can form a separate social network with each other apart from the rest of the family and the world. As such they often develop a private channel of communication between each other.

Twins frequently understand each other's immature speech, even when no one else can. They may have fluent utterances only understood by each other and perhaps another family member. They may have special words for things. The ability to communicate verbally outside of the family's language is called 'private language'.

The same twins who develop a separate way of communicating with each other have been found to have delayed language acquisition of the language of their family and culture. The suggested reason for this occurrence is with a private channel of communication, the twins have less need and desire to learn their culture's language. This suggests twins can develop a private social network of two, even more central to their existence than their families. Private languages like this are also found in siblings whose births are spaced closely to one another.

MZ twins are an even a more special case of a private social network. If mirroring behavior is how we learn social communication, then MZ twins hardly need to look at the other twin to mirror their behavior. They are virtually the same person at birth with the same genetic makeup and usually virtually the same history and environment. The difference between self-involvement and social communication must be a blurry line in this unique private social network of two. This must be a form of social/self-communication the rest of us can hardly imagine or understand. The bond between the MZ twins must be even stronger than the very strong bonds found within families and between DZ twins.

There is evidence that suggests MZ twins have more private language than DZ twins, but the numbers in the study were small and did not reach statistical significance. Private language, and the unusually close relationship between MZ twins, has been associated with poor language acquisition outcomes. Again, the idea is who needs to learn to communicate with the language of your culture if your little social network of two is so cozy and satisfying? However, in general, private language tends to disappear as the child grows up, even in MZ twins, as they enter the world around them.

For a moment accept my premise that two-way communication is vital for the development of normal social communication in a baby. MZ twins easily and effortlessly communicate with their identical mirror image playmate. Could that experience interfere with the need the twins have to socialize with the rest of the world? If so, might they have a tendency to develop ASD more frequently?

Might an excess of twin-to-twin communication be disruptive to the normal social communication development for MZ twins? If this is so, then all the prior twin studies have exaggerated the genetic cause of ASD and underestimated the effect of the child's experiences on this condition.

Recent Twin Study from California

About two months after this section was initially written, a large study including 192 twin pairs with strict autism and ASD was published from Stanford University by Hallmayer et al. The authors found a much larger rate of concordance for ASD and strict autism between DZ twins than in previous studies. The differences in the concordance rates between MZ and DZ were reduced compared to prior studies.

This study shows environmental factors are much more important than shown in prior twin studies and account for 57% of the cause of ASD and autism. Genetic factors are down to 38%. There are two possible reasons for this difference from the prior studies: one is either this study or the prior studies were wrong because of some methodological problems then or now.

The other possibility is an environmental factor or cause has become stronger over time. The earliest twin studies showed the cause of autism was 90% genetic. Now the latest studies show genetic factors are only 38%. Looking over the many twin studies that have been reported from then until now I think there has been a gradual tendency for the genetic contribution to lessen over this time period.

During this same period, the incidence of ASD has dramatically increased. Remember 50 years ago autism was a practically unknown disorder. It was still quite uncommon 35 years ago when the first twin studies were reported. The way I interpret this is 35 years ago, before the invasion of much one-way communication in the nursery, the nursery environment did not encourage ASD. Those children with ASD had it more on a genetic basis as the early twin studies showed.

Now more and more children are being pushed into ASD by one-way communication. Hence the most recent study shows a large environmental factor. Genetic factors alone are not strong enough by themselves to create more than a few children with ASD. Unfortunately, given the wrong environment, they are strong enough to make many children susceptible. The exposure to one-way communication has increased dramatically over the past 50 years and will be discussed more in Chapter Seven.

So this most recent study showed a large environmental influence on the development of a child with ASD. Even so, the authors remark that the model they used to estimate the relative influence of environment versus genetics assumes the environmental influences are the same for DZ and MZ twins. This, I believe, is wrong. MZ twins can form a very special case of a private social network which would tend to push both MZ twins together into ASD. If I am right, then the strength of the environmental contribution is still being underestimated, even in this new important study.

The early twin studies changed the entire direction of research for ASD. If you accept the idea that genetics has a major role to play in the causation of ASD, then the next question is: why and how does this happen? A minor industry has arisen to figure out the answer to this question.

The Role of Specific Genes in ASD

The twin studies we just discussed set off a kind of gold rush of studies looking for the genes that cause of ASD. With such a strong genetic association demonstrated by the early studies of twins with autism, it was thought in no time the genetic cause of ASD would be worked out.

First, let me state I am not a geneticist and the point of this book is not to make you an expert on the genetics of ASD either. This is an area filled with high technology and high hopes. As the instruments for analyzing our genome have become more and more capable, the understanding of how our genes affect our biochemistry and our development have become more detailed and sophisticated. Of course, the big hope is all this research will lead to the production of some medication which will help cure or treat the child with ASD.

With my apologies offered ahead of time, let me plunge into the genetics of ASD; the known and the unknown. First of all, what kind of genetic changes are we looking for to explain the cause of ASD? Everyone agrees the location of the problem is in the brain.

For any brain function there is a neural network, which is a shorthand way of describing a group of anatomic locations and pathways in the brain involved in the execution of that function. The same thing we referred to as a *trait* in the prior section, we are going to call a *brain function* in this section. A brain function corresponds to a trait located in the brain. Then how can a gene affect a certain brain function? To make things simple, there are three ways.

Genes and Anatomic Development

The first way a gene can affect a neural network is anatomically, by affecting the very architecture of the brain. Before birth, virtually all neurons (nerve cells) are formed, and under normal conditions at birth they have migrated to their proper positions in the brain. By that time, a huge number of neurons have been formed though conversely a huge number have died. Step by step, the proper anatomical structures have been created.

During infancy, head size, brain weight, and thickness of the outer layer of the brain dramatically increase. The outer layer of the brain is called the *cerebral cortex* and is where much of our mental activity takes place. The connections between neurons, which are called synapses, continue to increase until the approximate ages of 9 months to 2 years. At that point the infant or toddler has 50% more synapses than the adult.

Even after birth, many neurons continue to die. This process of neuronal death continues full bore until 2 years age, finally stopping about the age of seven. This incredible developmental process shapes the function and form of the brain. Since each step is built on the previous one, if something goes wrong early on, all subsequent steps may be thrown off.

An abnormal gene can cause the sequence of anatomic development to go awry. As a result, when we look at the brain either through some imaging technique such as an MRI during a patient's lifetime or at the time of autopsy, we can see actual physical structures that are too small, too big, in the wrong place, weakened, made of the wrong materials, etc. etc. The anticipated normal architecture of the brain is not present.

But there also must be enormous differences in the micro-anatomy of the brain from person to person. The way each synapse and each neuron is initially laid out in the brain is controlled genetically. Part of these genetic controls will allow our brains to be customized over time to fit to the needs of our bodies and our life. It is during the first and second year of life when we are introduced into our unique physical and social environment when most of the neuron death takes place. By this process and others, our brains are embedded into the world around us, prepared for future development and action.

Genes and Electro-biochemistry

The second way genes can affect how brain functions operate is *electro-biochemical*. I have added the *electro-* part unto the *biochemical* because so much of the brain's functioning is dependent on electricity. The electricity is generated by biochemical reactions. Just as we use electric signals to communicate rapidly, the brain does the same.

Much of the brain's volume consists of axons and their surrounding myelin sheaths along with supporting cells called glia. Axons are analogous to wires. Communication travels fast on axons from one part of the brain to another and throughout the rest of the body as nerve impulses, or tiny jolts of electricity. The myelin acts like insulation does on wires and allows for the faster conduction of these nerve impulses.

Myelin also serves to kind of hard-wire connections. Once myelin is in place, it is harder for the brain to rewire the connection. Unlike most animals, human brains are not born completely myelinated at birth. Myelin gradually develops throughout the brain over the course of childhood and adolescence. Even skills learned later in life may involve axons acquiring a myelin coating.

Dendrites receive the nerve impulses carried by axons at the next neuronal connection point. These connection points are called synapses. There are about 100 trillion synapses in the brain. Pure biochemical reactions occur at the synapses. Neurotransmitters are biochemicals that carry the signals across the synapses. They have such names as dopamine, acetylcholine, and serotonin and are involved with the action of many medications affecting the brain.

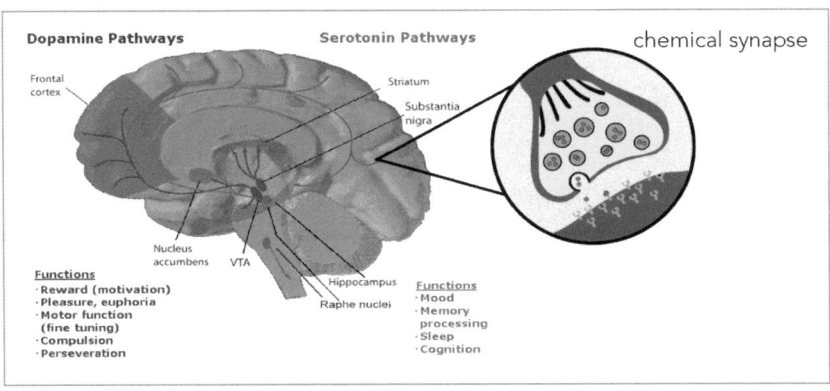

Just like the anatomical structures of the brain form connections and pathways, these neurotransmitters can form related pathways and systems. The reactions at the synapse are very fast but the effects are much more localized than nerve impulses which can go far and wide. A given neuron may have hundreds of dendrites all taking in the different signals from different synapses.

Getting back to genes, the function of these neurons with or without their myelin sheaths and their various neurotransmitters are ultimately governed by the biochemistry created by the activity of genes. If any one of these many genes malfunctions, there may be problems.

Genes and Brain Plasticity

The third way genes can affect the brain is through the interaction between anatomy and electro-biochemistry. Over time and with repetition, these instantaneous electro-biochemical reactions taking place in the neurons and their synapses will lead to actual anatomical changes in the brain itself. These changes take place from the level of the microscopic synapse all the way to large areas on the surface of the brain. The net effect is frequent neural activities become faster, more permanent and more energy efficient. They become overall more robust.

For instance, the pianist who practices day after day will end up a larger surface area of their brains dedicated to finger motions than mine. His speed and agility on the piano keyboard will be far beyond my capability. Playing a piece of music, something that would be quite impossible for me to perform, may seem virtually effortless to him.

Likewise, if you are born blind, the surface area of the brain devoted to vision will decrease while that devoted to hearing will increase. The anatomy of the brain will change with certain neural pathways becoming larger while others recede.

Or suppose you have a stroke and a piece of your brain dies. The anatomy and structure of your brain has changed irrevocably. That piece of the brain lost in the stroke can no longer work. Let us say as a result of this stroke you lose some brain function, such as moving your left little finger. You may recover that function, with training and time. That finger may not be as good as new, but it is now useful and operational. What has happened? Different areas of the brain have taken over the function that was performed in the part of the brain destroyed by the stroke.

As this change actually happens there must be countless changes of the brain's micro-anatomy at the level of neuron and its many synapses. The axons with their surrounding myelin sheaths have to change as well. These changes are triggered by the change in the pattern of electro-biochemical reactions in the brain.

In a way, your brain is customized for you by this process. This process of learning caused by repetition is called *Hebbian learning*. This learning takes place because repetitions of nerve impulses can actually cause changes in the brain's anatomy perhaps mediated by the glia. Again, getting back to genes, if a gene involved in this process is defective, problems may arise.

So when looking at the different genes that can lead to ASD, we may expect to find genes that affect the structure of the brain and how it develops, genes that affect the electro-biochemistry of the brain, or the interaction of both. Another way of looking at this is certain genes effect the formation and organization of the brain whiles others effect the operation. Finally there are the genes that orchestrate the interaction between structure and operation. All three types could conceivably be contributing to the genesis of ASD.

Getting Back to ASD

When the twin studies came out showing the strong association between genes and ASD, it was hoped that it would be an easy process to discover the autism gene, the gene that caused autism. The investigators would simply put together a group of people who had the phenotype for autism and analyze their genes for abnormalities compared to normal people. *Phenotype*, for our purposes, means the same thing as *trait* and *brain function* in the previous sections. Phenotype is the word geneticists use for observable traits. Unfortunately it has not proven easy to discover that pesky gene.

One of the great questions tantalizing the academics of the middle ages was how many angels could sit on the point of a pin. Today the question is how many genes does it takes to make a child autistic. In the twin studies we learned that the sub-traits, or the features that make up the phenotype of ASD, are distributed widely across any culture studied. This means very few people will carry all the features and likewise few people will have none of the features of the phenotype for ASD. Most of us are going to have some of the features to some degree.

In terms of genetics, this means several genes are going to be involved in the inheritance of this phenotype. If there were just one gene involved, then there would be basically be two groups: a group with all the features of the phenotype and a group with none. The spectrum nature of this phenotype (ASD) is strong evidence that at least 10 genes are involved, and perhaps there are hundreds of genes involved, each making a small contribution to the problem.

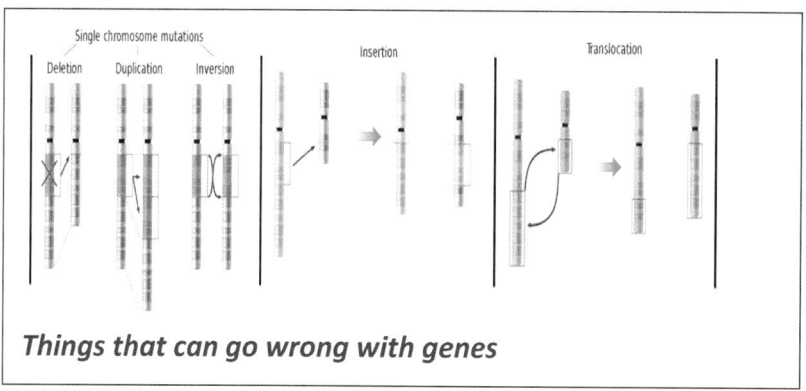

Things that can go wrong with genes

What happens to genes to cause these genetic problems? There is a long list of things that can go wrong with genes. There can be too much genetic material or there can be a loss of genetic material. The genetic material can be altered in a way that destroys or hampers its function. Again, I am going to apologize to you for not being a geneticist, but this area quickly gets very complicated. I am trying to keep it simple for you and I. The illustration above gives you a concise idea of what kinds of things can go wrong. That said, what have we learned about the genetic cause of ASD from these investigations?

Young girl with Rett's Syndrome

Syndromic Autism

The area where genetic studies have been most successfully linked to ASD is called *Syndromic Autism*. These studies look at groups of children who have different syndromes related to ASD. The syndromes have some features of ASD but also have distinctive features not a part of ASD. For instance, children with Fragile X syndrome have avoidance of eye contact, repetitive behaviors, inattention, and language acquisition delays; all features of ASD. Also as part of the syndrome, they have a characteristic facial appearance and low muscle tone which are unrelated to ASD.

A genetic change in the X chromosome causes this syndrome. There is a gene on the X chromosome with the name of FMR1. In Fragile X syndrome, there is extra material on this gene that interferes with its normal function. It is thought this gene malfunction affects neurons and how neurons connect to each other. About 2-6% of children with ASD are found to have Fragile X syndrome.

Likewise, children with *Rett's syndrome* have many features of ASD. Originally, the DSM-IV included Rett's syndrome as part of ASD. This syndrome is caused by mutations in the MECP2 gene. Approximately 1% of children diagnosed with ASD are found to have mutations in this gene.

However, the children with Rett's syndrome form a separate group with a different and distinctive phenotype than children with regular ASD. They have progressive gait disorders, decreased head growth, and hand wringing; features not found in ASD in general. For these reasons, they were pulled out of the ASD group in DSM-V. Nevertheless, they have a known gene abnormality that does cause a syndrome with many of the features of ASD.

There are many other syndromes with single gene abnormalities with some of the features of ASD. Usually these children have been evaluated in genetic clinics because of the many other problems, including mental retardation and other anatomic and biochemical problems. Interestingly, in this group of children, the sex ratio between boys and girl is closer to even than the ratio in children with regular ASD.

While these groups of children with syndromic autism form a very small portion of the hundreds of thousands of children with ASD, understanding the biology of these defective genes may someday help our understanding of ASD.

Candidate Genes and ASD

Another way to discover which genes are involved in ASD, is to look at the entire genotype of people with ASD. *Genotype* is a word used to describe the total genetic makeup of an organism; in our case, a human being. In this kind of study, investigators analyze the genotypes of people who have ASD or a certain sub-trait of ASD and compare their genotypes with hundreds or thousands of otherwise normal people. They look for differences between the two groups to find the genes involved in ASD.

Over the past 50 years the technology for analyzing genotypes has become more detailed, faster, cheaper, and easier to use. This is tied to the amazing computational abilities of modern-day computers. I think it is fair to say there has been a revolution in this technology in recent times. A gene found by one of these studies may be linked to sub-traits found in ASD. It is then called a *candidate gene*.

There is long list of candidate genes that are being studied at any time. With the current technology, new candidate genes appear all the time. Some candidate genes are thought to affect the functioning of synapses, the places where neurons meet and communicate. Others are involved in neurodevelopment, controlling some aspects of neuron migration and brain development. Some affect the electro-biochemistry of the cells, for instance, altering the channels that sodium or calcium ions pass in or out of neurons. These candidate genes affect a broad array of processes in the brain that we might suspect to contribute to the cause of ASD.

There are new studies appearing all the time. One recent study from UCLA used the age the child speaks his first word as the trait, phenotype, or brain function (whatever terminology you prefer). This trait was then linked to a gene called CNTNAP2. The gene seems to influence the development of the brain structures involved with language. In other words, it influences the actual anatomy of the area of the brain involved with communication. Another recent study from John Hopkins University implicated a different gene called GRIP1 that affects social communication as well. The list of candidate genes grows longer all the time.

Discussion of the Role of Genetics in ASD

All in all, the twin studies are convincing for the role of a genetic predisposition in the development of ASD. Could this be the whole story? It is clearly not. I will argue one-way and two-way communication play a major role in the formation of ASD. The social networks we are born into shape which capabilities our brains will develop and which will not and this includes ASD.

Genetics will determine the potential ability we have for any brain function. But our social network will determine whether the ability develops or not. Simply put, the genes are the seeds and the social environment is the soil, the water, and sunlight. The social network determines the social environment the infant will face in the nursery.

The Trait under Question: *Ability to hit a Baseball*
The Question: *Is this Trait Genetic?*
Or is it Acquired?

The First study:
As baseball is first introduced into a culture for the first time.

Dizygotic concordance 50%
Batting Averages:
Twin one: .010
Twin two: .002

Monozygotic concordance 90%
Batting Averages:
Twin three: .009
Twin four: .008

Both DZ and MZ twins can barely hit the ball. Study 1 concludes: The big difference in Concordance between MZ and DZ twins shows the trait is 90% Genetic.

The Second study:
10 years later: The culture has changed. Everyone is batting better.

Dizygotic concordance 50%
Batting Averages:
Twin one: .200
Twin two: .250

Monozygotic concordance 90%
Batting Averages:
Twin three: .225
Twin four: .220

Both DZ and MZ twins play pretty well now. Study 2 concludes: The big difference in Concordance between MZ and DZ twins shows the trait is 90% Genetic, again.

But, doesn't the big difference between Study 1 and Study 2 show the trait is also *acquired*.

Conclusion: A trait like ASD can show a strong linkage to both genetics and environmental forces.

Take, for instance, the ability to hit with a bat with a ball that is pitched to you. For those of you who live in a culture without baseball, the analogy works the same with soccer and ball kicking. Imagine there is a place where no one has heard of such a thing as baseball, and you are interested in introducing baseball to the people who live there.

So you go there and test 10-year-old boys on their ability to hit the ball. There will be a few boys who are pretty good the first time they try, many so-so, and a few are abysmal. You will probably note that the identical twins who live there will have very high concordance; that is to say, each identical twin will have almost the same ability to hit the ball.

When you test the fraternal twins will find one of these twins will be a better hitter than the other just like any other two brothers might be. You would note the concordance between the MZ twins is much higher than the DZ twins. You would conclude at this point, and rightly so, the ability to hit the ball is primarily genetic. In order words, the cause of the trait we are describing is genetic.

Now, 10 years later, you return and your project to introduce baseball has become wildly successful. Everyone in this culture now loves the new game. All baby boys are born with little baseball bats placed in their cribs. Everyone is learning about baseball; how to swing a bat, catch a ball, when to bunt and so on. They are watching other people playing baseball and seeing how the best players swing at the ball.

You are delighted with the change. You return and perform the same study as you did before. This time your 10-year-olds are hitting the ball much better than ten years ago. You are amazed how much better they are. Then you test the 10 year old MZ and DZ twins to see if the ability to hit the ball in baseball still is primarily genetic or not.

Guess what, the concordance rate between MZ twins is still much higher than DZ twins. From these studies, you still conclude this trait for ball hitting is controlled by genetic factors. You may conclude environmental factors are not important. But then how do you explain why all the boys in this culture are hitting so much better?

The point is pervasive changes in a culture over time can shift the entire curve for any trait that involves learning in one direction or another. The potential to develop that trait in any one individual will largely be determined by their genetic makeup or their genotype. Whether they actually develop the trait is still determined largely by the social network they grow up in.

This rule applies to the traits found in children with ASD. The fundamental problem in ASD is the failure of social communication. Something has changed in our cultural environment that is impacting the development of this trait. Something is shifting the curve towards self-involvement and self-stimulation.

The change is truly worldwide. This change is impacting the development of social communication during the critical first year of life. It is this shift in the curve that is causing ASD to become so much more prevalent. Nothing genetic has changed. The genotypes in the population as a whole are virtually the same as fifty years ago.

Genetics underlies the propensity for any one child to have more or less interest in self-involvement over social communication. But the role of the family and the culture in the shaping of the environment of the baby can hardly be overlooked. In the next chapter, I will look at how the social environment, by itself, can cause ASD even without any special genetic predisposition.

About Otto – Six
Rosangela's Stories- Three

When Otto went for his flu shot the nurses immobilized him. They held him strongly and gave him the shot. As soon as he got free from the nurses he ran from the room towards the street. Aware of the dangers of Otto's behavior; Marcio stopped him from leaving the building, trying to keep him inside of the waiting room. Upset, Otto decided then, in front of everyone, to take his clothes off.

Marcio's first quick reaction was to grab Otto and throw him inside of the car. I asked Marcio to go and take care of Erik. I called Otto, who was naked, and told him that I would run on the streets with him if he wanted. I invited him to run very fast and to the farthest that we could.

He then accepted my invitation. Then I added that the condition for us to run was to be properly dressed with clothes and shoes. He agreed. I dressed him up and we ran towards the street holding hands. We ran for a long time. Finally, then Otto said that we had run enough and we came back talking normally. Otto had calmed down.

I noticed that Otto had a need to cry. Otto had difficulty in expressing his feelings, his anger, his pain, and his stress. I thought that all those feelings in having a vaccine could be relieved with a good cry. Otto was missing this knowledge. When Otto would get hurt he would not cry. He would become very angry and aggressive.

So, I started teaching him to cry. I would show him sad movies (Disney movies always have some sad part, or this cartoon song sang by a little doll named Xuxa that is also very sad). When I could observe his attention and understanding of the movie I would encourage him to cry. We would cry together, I had no problem in doing that. I would invite Otto to cry with me, telling him that the situation being shown in the movie was very sad.

The first time Otto cried during the movie it was a strongly felt cry, he was sobbing. Marcio and I had an argument. I expressed my opinion to him. I thought that it was necessary to teach Otto how to cry. In my opinion if Otto could learn that frustrations could be relieved with crying then he would not be as aggressive as he was anymore.

Since then Otto cries more frequently. He cries when he gets hurt, when he cannot get what he wants, when he fights with his brother, and I believe he found a better way to express himself.

- Rosangela Eichler

Author's Comment

Both parents find Otto's undressing unacceptable and probably find it embarrassing. Marcio takes a physical approach to solving the problem. Rosangel tries to understand Otto's intentions and demonstrates her empathy by running with him.

Chapter Six
Social Environment

I have written about the gender-related and genetic causes of ASD in the previous two chapters. Both topics focus on the inborn genetic tendency to develop ASD.

But what about the world that surrounds the infant and toddler? What influence does it have on a child who is developing ASD? In the next two chapters I will discuss the opposite side of the coin. I will show how the social environment and communication during infancy can affect whether a child will actually develop ASD. In this chapter, I will show how social experiences by themselves without any special genetic predisposition can cause ASD or at least disrupt social relationships.

Going back to our model on brain functions from Chapter Three, there are two periods of time the brain can interact with the environment to learn a new brain function. The first is the critical period, the optimum time to acquire and develop a new capability. This is the developmental stage when the brain is primed and ready to learn that brain function. However, the brain still needs the right stimuli coming from the environment during the critical period to develop this function.

Past this time, the brain can often still acquire a certain function by a process called *brain plasticity*. It takes more effort, practice, and time for the brain to learn this new function after the critical period, much like learning a second language later in life.

This chapter is therefore about what happens when the critical period for learning social communication is disrupted by severe neglect. The next chapter will talk about what happens when the same critical period is disrupted by a flood of one-way communication brought into the nursery by the Pied Pipers of Autism. The Pied Pipers of Autism are TV, video, video devices and toys that speak. This flood of one-way communication is causing the rapid increase in ASD, but again, I am getting ahead of myself.

Social communication is such a basic need for infants we all know almost intuitively babies need human attention, usually from their mothers. A baby without a mother brings out very strong maternal feelings in both men and women. A crying baby begs to be held, handled, and comforted.

Sometimes a baby will be socially isolated within its own family. In these cases there is usually abuse, malnutrition or at the very least a bizarre family configuration. Sad as it is, sometimes, albeit rarely, an otherwise normal baby will not be wanted and will be adopted out of the protection of its natural family. In certain places such a foundling might end up in an institution where babies are socially isolated but otherwise fairly well taken care of.

For over a hundred years our culture has believed and known this practice is very bad for children, so fortunately there are relatively few children with this experience. We will be looking at some of these unfortunate children and what we can learn about ASD from them.

Social Isolation in Monkeys

Monkey returned to social network after isolation remains socially isolated.

Before we get to these children, let us look at some experiments done with monkeys dealing with the effects of social isolation. At the time these experiments were done, in the 1950s and 1960s at the University of Wisconsin by Dr. H. Harlow, the effects of maternal and social deprivation were at best poorly understood. The cultural belief that holding a baby too much would spoil the child was widespread.

At the time in academia the then dominant behaviorist school of psychology believed the mother-baby relationship was no more than behavior learned by a series of rewards and punishments. They also believed the most important factor forming the mother-baby bond was the reward of milk.

The experiments proved this idea wrong by showing baby monkeys preferred a wire-frame model of a mother covered with cloth to a wire-frame model of a mother with a bottle of milk attached. In the experiments, the baby monkeys were isolated from their natural mothers and the rest of their social group.

These were very sad experiments. The experimenter found these completely socially isolated baby monkeys had great difficulties returning to their social group. Later on, other studies were done with partial and complete social isolation. The baby monkeys in these experiments were given adequate provisions to grow but no contact or limited contact with other monkeys.

For instance in one experiment, during the first 6 months of life a baby monkey could watch the other monkeys playing and interacting through a window but could not participate. In other words they were connected to the other monkeys by observation only (one-way communication).

These poor monkeys developed abnormalities such as blank staring, repetitive motions, and self-mutilation. These are all behaviors found in ASD. The researchers described the socially isolated monkeys as being *autistic-like* when they were re-introduced into monkey society. They were self-absorbed and socially inept. If the monkeys were isolated from birth to six months, these changes were almost entirely irreversible.

They often just rocked back and forth alone. They had extremely inappropriate behaviors for their social networks. By and large, they were unable to form normal relationships with the other monkeys. Nothing the experimenter tried to restore these monkeys back to social health helped. The only exception was when the researcher exposed young monkeys who had been socially isolated for 6 months to normal monkeys who were three months younger.

Monkeys are very social animals with well-developed social behavior very similar to humans. These studies demonstrated the disruption of the critical period for learning social communication in monkeys by social isolation produced a constellation of behaviors also found in humans with ASD.

These were presumably normal monkeys without any special genetic predisposition to these behaviors. It is hard, thank goodness, to find children socially isolated like these monkeys were. However, these experiments show the failure to develop social communication can arise from an environmental cause alone, no genetics needed.

Infants in Institutions

Infant in orphanage in Romania

In Romania, during the time of the dictator Ceausescu (1967-1989), birth control was forbidden. As a result there were many unwanted babies born. They were often placed in foundling nurseries.

These nurseries were set up with 20 to 30 infants per caregiver. Often the infants were confined to their cribs or cots, with few or no toys to play with or other activities. Feeding, washing, and changing were done as a group. There was no time or expectation for human interaction for these unfortunate infants. These children were deprived of social contact during this first year of life. What happened to them?

Many were later adopted by families in Western countries and many studies have been done to assess the effects of early deprivation on language, cognitive ability (IQ), and socialization.

Many of these children had findings of ASD and with the full range of features found in ASD, from difficulty with social communication to repetitive motions. Like the monkeys, many of the children rocked as a form of self-comfort. Many of the children had sensory disturbances, such as craving the feel of some cloth.

They were described as being without empathy, resistant to human contact, and prone to retreat in to their own worlds. They were also subject to temper tantrums. So again, like the monkeys, a severely disturbed environment that lacks almost all social communication during the first year of life can produce a child with the features of ASD.

There is no reason to believe these children had an unusual inherent tendency to develop ASD. It is not surprising this social environment produces children with ASD. If excessive self-involvement is producing the symptoms of ASD, then growing up in an institution like this almost forces self-involvement.

A third example of extreme social isolation is a phenomenon known as *feral children*. These are children who for a variety of reasons grow up without human contact and are found later in life.

Feral Child

Often they are found after the critical period for language acquisition has passed and they are never able, or interested in, developing that capability. They are also described as *autistic-like*, with inabilities to ever gain facility in language or human social communications. They are self-absorbed, resistant to human contact, and have sensory disturbances such as being indifferent to pain. Many times feral children have been found living in the wild as part of a social group of animals. Those found are often torn from their animal social network, usually without any good effects.

Blindness and Deafness

As these previous examples demonstrate, complete social isolation will often produce a child with the traits of ASD. Let me be clear: *complete social isolation by itself can cause ASD or at least major disruption in future social relations.* But what about lesser degrees of social isolation? The situation with children who are born completely blind, I think, is instructive in this context. Children born with even minimal eyesight or who become blind at a later age do not have problems with social communication. But those children born totally blind from birth, these children as infants will experience some degree of social isolation.

The problem is so many social stimuli are carried to infants through the medium of sight. Facial expressions, body language, and, very importantly, eye contact are all missing for these children from birth. With the loss of eye contact comes the loss of joint attention experiences. As a result they have delayed social development and understanding.

Some of the blind children with low cognitive abilities (low IQ's) will develop repetitive movements, but the children with normal intelligence do not develop any of the traits associated with excessive self-involvement.

However, they often do have difficulties with social communication and do not develop a theory of mind until much later than children with normal sight. A theory of mind refers to the ability to 'mind read' other people. Joint attention is also delayed, but language is acquired normally.

So blindness helps tease out some of the different features of ASD. First, it demonstrates again manifestations of self-involvement are different depending on the cognitive ability (IQ) of the child. Secondly, as in the Asperger's form of ASD, it shows language and social communication skills can follow a different course from each other. Loss of exposure to visual social cues can interfere with the acquisition of social communication but does not interfere with the learning of a spoken language.

Overall, the experience of congenitally blind children shows social communication is at least partially learned. No genes are needed to produce these traits of ASD, just a form of social isolation during the first year of life.

Deaf children have a different problem. They see all the normal social clues but they cannot hear or learn spoken language. They have a different form of social isolation on this basis. If a family member knows sign language, they quickly adapt and their social development becomes entirely normal. Otherwise, deaf children may have difficulties with social development as well, in this case centered on language.

Helen Keller's story is described in her autobiography, *The Story of My Life*. She had normal hearing, vision and behavior until she was 19 months old when an illness left her blind and deaf. After this illness, she became more or less socially isolated, locked into her own world. She and another child living in her house shared a limited private sign language. During this time her behavior resembled that of a child with ASD.

Later on, after long hours of attention by her tutor and lifelong friend Anne Sullivan, she had a break through joint attention experience, shared by means of touch, while learning the word for water in sign language. With that experience, the channel of communication provided by sign language opened up for her. From there she went on to a distinguished life full of education and accomplishments.

This fascinating story has been dramatized again and again. It shows social isolation can lead to an ASD-like picture even when it starts at 19 months of age. It also shows human dedication and attention can re-open channels of communication with such a child and thereby reverse ASD in all or in part.

All these situations I have talked about so far in this chapter show how deprivation of social communication in infants and toddlers can lead otherwise genetically normal children to develop all or some of the features of ASD. However, the outlook for these children may be better than for those children who develop autism because of a strong genetic predisposition. All in all, these examples show the social environment of the infant can be at least as important for the development of ASD as the child's genetic make up.

Infancy- The Critical Period for Social Communication

What evidence is there that the first year of life is the critical period to establish social communication? During a critical period the brain is prepared to acquire a certain function. A craving or a need-state develops to search the surrounding world for whatever is needed to learn this function. Acquisition of this function is easy, appearing at times almost effortless. This certainly seems to be the case for human infants and social interaction during the first year of life.

Some of the brain functions required for social communication include facial recognition, eye contact, pointing, joint attention, language comprehension, language expression, social imitation, the ability to form a theory of mind of the other person, shared pretending, and other functions.

All these functions develop during the first years of life and they usually develop in a certain order. This is no accident. The order of development is determined by the need for one brain function to be operational before the next brain function can form. They all act together to help us express our intentions, share our experiences, understand the intentions of other people and in the end, coordinate our actions.

Disturbances early on in this sequence of development can lead to failure later on. Infants at two months of age react to the attention of their caregivers. They may smile or they may avoid a gaze, but they react. This early reaction shows infants of this age have discovered there are other people in this world with them. By four months, they may make sounds to attract our attention. They have developed awareness their actions can attract social interactions.

These are the beginnings of social communication and will lead directly into the start of joint attention. If one step in this chain of developmental milestones fails to happen, the next step cannot occur either.

This is a problem in ASD. The developmental sequence for social communication is disturbed in infancy but the consequences usually are not noted until there is failure of speech, one or two years later. Fortunately, we are learning to detect these disturbances at an earlier age, even during the first year of life. By the second year of life, the signs of ASD are routinely noted by astute and experienced clinicians.

We can never forget the importance of social communication in our lives and in the lives of our babies. Establishing social communication in a family social network is crucial to the development of trust and security in the infant. As humans, our basic needs are *oxygen, water, fuel, and social interaction,* in that order.

Language Acquisition

Language acquisition is linked to social communication. Children with the more severe side of autism fail to develop language skills. Understanding how language is acquired can help us understand how social communication is acquired as well.

Language acquisition is the process by which humans develop the capacity to understand, produce, and use words to communicate. This process involves learning the grammar, the phonology (the sounds), and the vocabulary of a language shared by a network of other speakers; the various parts of language relate to one another to form a whole. The process is the same for children learning sign language.

Children acquire language quickly, easily and with little effort or formal instruction. They learn automatically, by observation and imitation, whether their parents try to teach them or not. Although the people in their families do not set out to teach their children to speak, they do perform a vital role by talking to their infants, toddlers, and children.

Children who are not engaged in two-way communication (conversation) will not acquire language. Language must be used for social interactions with the child; for example, a child who regularly hears language on the TV or radio but nowhere else will not learn to talk.

Scaffolding and development of Language Acquisition

13-18 years Total fluency in native language.

7-13 years Greater fluency and competence. Gradual loss of ability to acquire fluency in non native language.

4-7 years Complex sentences grows; Asks questions. uses past tense; vocabulary to 1,500 words or more. grammar almost entirely normal.

2-4 years More complex sentences; vocabulary grows rapidly; likes being read to; grammar improves; speech clear.

1-2 years Speech emerges. From one word to phrases; comprehension grows; understands commands; vocabulary grows.

6-12 months Comprehension of native language appears. Ignores non-native language sounds; Make repetitive sounds of native language.

3-6 months Babbling; Imitation of native language sounds; Motherese with reciprocal imitation.

1-3 months Watching lips. Preference for sounds of native language; cooing; soothed by singing.

Three Steps to Learning Language

The following three steps are crucial for language acquisition as well as the overall development of general communication skills:

1) **Attending and Looking**: This is the first step to learning language. Two-way communication by eye contact opens a reciprocal channel of communication for the young infant and the caregiver/mother. Eye contact is a fundamental brain function whose importance in establishing two-way communication can hardly be exaggerated. Babies will start seeking eye contact as early as four weeks after birth. The babies will have a tendency to stare at the mouths of adults during

speech production. Blind children have been shown to make 'eye' contact by attending to the localization of mother's voice.

2) **Expressions of Emotion:** The crying and cooing behaviors of the infant elicit specific responses in the mother and caregivers. This is the start of the rewards the baby will get for communication. It earns them the pleasure of mother's milk, caresses, and attention. Babies relish the company and the talk of their caregivers and need these things to establish communication. The baby will be rewarded, comforted, and protected by its family. This is the beginning of the process of forming the bond between the baby and their family.

Steps one and two happen before the next step in the development of communication. Imitation builds on the prior formation of a meaningful reciprocal channel of communication between the caregiver/mother and baby. Language acquisition, even at this early stage, is a series of steps, one building on the other.

3) **Reciprocal Imitation:** Starting at three months, a phenomenon known as *turn-taking* occurs whereby the caregiver/mother and the baby take turns mimicking each other's vocalizations. It is by imitation the infant learns the language from their mother and family. This period of language acquisition is defined by the interaction between baby talk and Motherese.

> Motherese is a way of talking to babies found in mothers everywhere. The mother will use a special tone, pace, intonation, and accent that makes speech easier to understand. Baby talk is the infant's approximation of Motherese as the infant tries to mimic the mother. In the first year of life a profound amount of this kind of interaction is required for the infant to learn language.

The first sounds a baby makes are the sounds of crying; they are usually very good at this. The ability to cry is certainly an inherent ability. Mothers have the reciprocal inherent ability to recognize their own baby's cry. Within 48 hours mothers can recognize their own baby's cry from any other baby.

By about six weeks of age, the baby starts making vowel sounds, starting with *ahh*, *ee*, and ooh. At about six months of age, the baby starts to produce consonant-vowel pair sounds such as boo and da. The baby is sorting out which sounds are important in the family's language. A parent may hear "mama" or "dada" at this age, but at this point the baby assigns no meaning to this utterance.

It is hard to study how much language the baby understands at this point. We can assume receptive language (understanding) is far ahead of expressive language. After all, humans are born with the ability to hear but only learn to control the spoken language organs, such as the larynx, tongue, and mouth, much later.

Many families are introducing sign language into the life of their baby as early as six months of age. Two months later these infants can be shown to be signing back to their parents. This clearly demonstrates expressive language can be produced by infants even during the first year of life. The challenge of learning sign language is much greater for the adult, who is usually well past their critical period for learning a new language.

Somewhere around the age of one to one and a half, the child will actually begin to say single words with meanings such as "cookie" or "doggie." During this time, they will start to follow simple commands, demonstrating their understanding of many of the words they have been hearing and of the inflection of the voice at the end of a question sentence. This inflection is found in all Indo-European languages.

This understanding also shows they realize words represent things. It will take another year before they start to combine words. This is part of the developmental order for acquiring language. Around the age of two, they start making two-word sentences. By this time, Motherese is long gone, and the toddler can understand adult speech fairly well.

All normal children who grow up in a normal family and consequently are surrounded by conversation will acquire the language of their family.

There is an area in the cerebral cortex of the brain for understanding spoken language. This area surrounds the area for hearing. It is no surprise a brain function this important and complex has an actual physical location large enough to be mapped and consistently placed in normal human brains.

As with any brain function of sufficient importance language acquisition has been studied genetically. There are known genes affecting this process. For instance, there is gene called FOXP2 that is vital to language production and is only found in humans.

When humans have acquired the ability to speak a language to the level of a native speaker, they are said to have reached *peak proficiency*. There is a decline of proficiency of acquiring a new language with increasing age of first exposure after the age of four to six.

There is a range of inherent abilities in the population for this brain function as well. My own son first learned French when he was sixteen years old and after one year of living in France, native speakers were not able to discern that he was not a native speaker himself. But for most people, they will never be able to achieve peak proficiency in a language acquired after the age of six to ten.

Mothering

One thing we can conclude from this discussion is mothering is critically important to learning both language and social communication. It prepares the child to participate in the different social networks he will encounter in life. I am using the word "mother" in the broad sense of a human who has repetitive caring and attentive interactions with the baby; it could very well be the father as well.

Mothering certainly means more than providing milk for the baby. It is also a set of caregiver's behaviors that serve to bind the newborn to its family and culture. The caregiver sets up a model for the baby to imitate. Normal maternal behavior in all cultures involves lots of face-to-face contact with the baby and Motherese as we previously discussed. Could there be a group of genes controlling this brain function in the mother or is it learned by imitation?

To be sure, breastfeeding is part of our genetic heritage as mammals. Just as sure, breast feeding is in part learned by imitation, by watching others do it. For a while, thanks to clever marketing, breastfeeding almost disappeared from our culture. To re-establish breastfeeding in our culture with mothers who had never seen anyone breastfeed before was a real challenge.

Challenges of Mothering in the Modern Age

Is there a certain optimal period of time in the mother's life for the development of the capability of mothering? We talk about teen mothers not being prepared for motherhood. In my experience, I have seen many immature, self-centered teenagers turn into capable mothers during the course of their pregnancy with the birth of their babies.

Could the birth of a baby trigger some inherent developmental sequence in the mother that lies dormant until then? Certainly during pregnancy and at the time of birth, there is production of a range of hormones known that could affect the brain of the mother.

What about a mother who is used to having a challenging career? How will they react to the slow pace of an infant? Will the infant hold their interest? Will they automatically be able to shift gears and get real pleasure from communication with their baby when they are used to multitasking on their computers and smart phones all day?

And then, what about the important social networks the mother is a part of? What if they view mothering as not as important as accomplishments outside of the home? What if the spouse can't be relied on to support the mother and baby? What if the mother's immediate social network is absent, distant, or toxic? What effect will this have on the quality of the mother's interactions with their infant? What if the mother is constantly distracted by other activities such as watching television, responding to smart phones, or the demands of work? These are all important questions I will not attempt to answer.

It can be argued the primary purpose of any social network is to reproduce. Any social network that does not reproduce will only disappear. It follows then the most important function of a social network is to provide an environment in which the infant and mother can thrive, especially during the critical years when a child is an infant or a toddler.

It seems to me during this very important period of life, mothers would benefit from attentive and supportive face-to-face relationships. Husbands and partners are great, but nuclear families are such small social networks. Do all mothers today belong to a larger social network that can provide that kind of attention? If not, what can or should be done? In this country, different religions, to their credit, try to provide this attention and support for their members who are having babies.

In this chapter we talked about how language and social communications are acquired in a series of behavioral steps with each step requiring a meaningful social interaction and building on the prior steps. We demonstrated presumably genetically normal infants who are socially deprived during the first year of life can develop ASD, on this basis only. We also discussed the challenges caregivers face in today's cultural environment.

But social deprivation is not the cause of the surge in the number of children who are developing ASD today. These are, by and large, children who are wanted, loved and certainly not neglected. The problem transcends any individual mother's behavior and rather reflects an ubiquitous and enormous change in the way infants are brought up in our modern culture.

Infants can be pushed into ASD by lack of social interaction or they can be pulled into ASD by the Pied Pipers of Autism namely television, videos, video devices and talking toys. The next chapter talks about the gradual but radical changes in the typical life of today's infants from a mere fifty years ago, when the incidence of ASD was 2,500% less than it is today.

Chapter Seven
Television, Video and Toys

Giovanna is my young daughter 18 months old at the time this book is being written. When she sees me using the computer she pleads with me, using body language and the few words she knows, to turn on YouTube so she can watch the videos she truly adores. Infants and toddlers are fascinated by video devices.

It is cute and harmless? After all, is she not learning language and getting a real window into our culture by watching these shows? Does it not offer the younger set both education and entertainment giving them a head start on a life of learning? At the same time, does it not also offer peace and quiet for the parents, so they can do the things they enjoy such as watching TV, surfing the internet, or playing video games or the things they have to do such as caring for their family and preparing for the next day of work.

The critical time for learning social communication is during the first year of life, as was discussed in Chapter 6. Babies are born interested in faces. They are looking for their moms. They can distinguish their mother's face from all others when they are just two days old. Likewise, mothers can distinguish their baby's cry from all others. Both are ready to connect one to the other to form the most important social relationship of the baby's life.

Later on, in this first year of life, infants will be attracted to other features in their environment that serve to identify people with whom they can interact. Infants pay attention to movements and voices from a very young age. These features help the infant distinguish objects from living beings and people, a fundamental and important separation.

In an infant's world, objects stay still until a living being, such as his caregiver, moves them. They learn physical forces control the movement of objects, while living beings move on the basis of some internal intention, not always easily understood. The infant learns by watching how things move in the space around them which things are living and which are objects.

This was a simple distinction until the arrival of video devices, such as television, into the nursery. Images on the video screen confuse the infant since they move like living things but are not really alive. The movements of the image seem to be controlled by some internal intention, but there is no social communication or interaction possible with a video device. For the purposes of learning social behavior, they are a dead end.

Voices serve to mark and identify people as being different from both objects and other living beings in the infant's world. The infant has an inborn attraction to the sounds of the language the people around him use. Sing to an infant and he is comforted and enchanted. Again, this acts like a beacon attracting the infant to form and develop social communication and relationships with the singer or talker. When the voice comes out of a talking toy, he ends up being attracted to another social dead end. The infant may enjoy listening to the toy's voice but this kind of interaction only serves to increase self-involvement.

As we have already seen in the prior chapter babies who do not have an adequate socialization with their caregivers can develop ASD on this basis alone. They can be more or less driven into self-communication and self-involvement by neglect.

There is another way to form children with ASD: during the first year of life, if self-involvement is so interesting and satisfying, the baby will turn away from social communication and end up on the path to developing ASD. They turn away from the complications of human relationships to the pleasures of self-stimulation. This sets in place a cascade of developmental events eventually leading to all the symptoms and traits of ASD. This is the environmental side of the Integrated Theory of Autism.

This chapter will discuss the radical changes in babies' experiences during the first year of life that have taken place over the past fifty years or so. I will show that these changes in how we raise our infants are an important cause of the increasing prevalence of ASD.

I will take the position that anything standing in the way physically, acoustically or visually between the baby and its caregivers, gets in the way of developing two-way communication and thereby encourages self-involvement in the baby. Any object that mimics the cues infants use to find social partners will seriously interfere with the infant's social development. This mimicry also serves to confuse certain babies and infants keeping them from forming a clear distinction between objects and people.

I will further make the argument babies are increasingly exposed in the nursery to objects which only provide one-way communication. One-way communication is the opposite of the back and forth exchanges of attention and eye contact found in two-way communication. Two-way communication is needed for joint attention and to form any and all social relationships.

Watching television or a video device, for example, is one-way communication. The baby pays attention to the television or video but the television or video pays *no* attention back to the baby. I know that is an obvious statement but it is critical for understanding why one-way communication is just another form self-communication and self-stimulation.

I will further state that no technological device can ever take the place of real attention from live people in raising our children. It takes loving attention to teach the vital skill of two-way communication to our infants. This need for attention never stops as our children grow up. Teachers and caregivers your jobs are safe.

Like the Pied Piper on Hamelin, slick one-way communication enchants our babies and takes them away from getting attention from, or giving attention to, the members of their families. A baby so enchanted never learns how to participate in his family's social network.

In the chapter that follows, I will demonstrate that one-way communication is becoming more and more intrusive into the nursery and life of the modern infant and toddler, and that this change corresponds with the increasing prevalence of ASD.

Toys

Fifty years ago, babies did not have many toys. Toys were considered a kind of luxury item, not the top priority in a family's budget. The idea babies needed to be taught anything 'educational' was not a part of the culture. A rattle was common toy, maybe a doll or two for the girls, but that was it. Cribs were unadorned.

Crib Toys

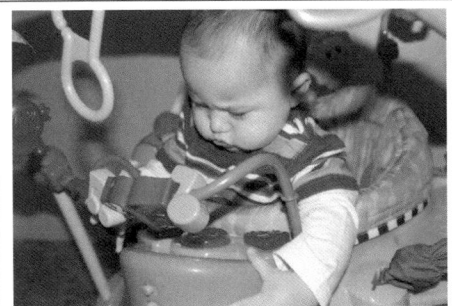

Baby trapped in a walker that features music, "computerese", faces, and colorful shapes that move and block the baby from being able to see his caregiver. He is gazing at a mirror.

Baby toys are ubiquitous today. The toys are cleverly designed and mass-produced. They are marketed in magazines aimed at new mothers and on television as well. They are relatively inexpensive. They promise to hold the infant's attention and they do. They promise to make the baby smarter and they don't.

They take up prime space around the baby. Today babies are surrounded in their cribs by toys of all shapes and colors competing for their visual attention. Where are the mother and the family in this picture? She is probably sitting somewhere in the distance behind this row of distraction. The toys have bright colors, make sounds even music, and easily move. The colors, the sounds, and the movements attract the attention and affection of the baby.

For some babies (especially boys), the toys are more interesting and fun than the mother's face and her company. Might some babies get confused on what or who is really important? When did crib toys and other such toys become so widespread for infants? The answer is within the last 20-30 years.

Talking Toys

The first talking toy was introduced in 1978 using a chip created by Texas Instruments. It was called 'Speak and Spell' and was aimed at older children. Over time the sound quality these chips could produce improved and the prices became less expensive. The chips are now found in many toys and millions and millions of these talking toys have been sold. They are extraordinarily common, even in the nursery.

As a baby gets older, say six months old, they are beset by talking toys. This is the age of Motherese and baby talk. The special higher tone of voice, exaggerated intonation, and slower tempo that all mothers everywhere use to talk with their baby is called Motherese. Presumably this behavior has been selected during the course of evolution to help form the connection between the mother and the baby. The baby is reciprocally ready to attend to the sound of their mother's talk and responds with pleasure and baby talk. The mother's voice has a special role at this time in life, capturing the baby's attention, strengthening the emotional bond between baby and caregiver, and introducing language.

This inborn process for eons has bonded baby to mother now has been hijacked by toy manufacturers. Toy manufacturers play close attention to what attracts the interest of the consumer, in this case babies. Advertising on television and some clever colorful packaging to attract the eyes of the caregiver and the baby is the first step. The toy needs to be noticed on the shelves of the store. If the baby seems amused by the toy in the store, there is a good chance it will end up in the shopping cart leaving the store.

At this age, babies are set to learn the sounds of the language of the most important social network in their life, their family. Instead, with these toys, they are listening to a synthetic voice; let's call it

Computerese. Between six months and one year is the critical period for the infant to learn the sounds of language. They imitate and learn to pay peak attention to the language they hear. They watch how our lips move as we talk. After one year, babies stop showing interest in vocal sounds not in their language.

Learning a language for a baby is normally a reciprocal face-to-face, back and forth process. The baby is making a social connection as well as learning to understand language. This learning happens very rapidly because the brain is in its critical periods for learning the sounds of spoken language.

The baby learns how to talk through observation and imitation and he learns to understand through countless episodes of joint attention with his mother and other family members. The infant gets pleasurably rewarded for the effort it takes to learn language by the social rewards of touches, eye contact, and the mother's special voice: Motherese. The mother gets rewarded by the babies' attention and cooing.

Now suppose instead the baby is spending its limited waking time listening to a toy talk Computerese. Will the baby attend to this pseudo-voice? Of course, they are virtually programmed to pay peak attention to voices at this age. Will they be engaged in a social two-way conversation with their caregiver or a one-way conversation with themselves? Well, there is nothing social about listening to a toy make language sounds. It will be one-way communication, not a conversation. The pleasure the baby gets from listening to the toy talk will reinforce self-involvement. The infant might even try to imitate the toy; the start of object-people confusion.

Take an infant, who for some reason, perhaps genetic, did not make a strong connection with his caregiver during the first six months of life, and place it with this talking toy. This infant might find the toy very interesting, just as pleasurable as listening to Mom and a lot simpler than learning their role in the human conversation.

As I said before, talking toys are ubiquitous. As the infant grows, they will find more and more of these disembodied voices trying to engage them in a sad parody of conversation. I suppose the reason the voices of these machines often produce sentences with the intonation of a question is to encourage child-machine interactions. Can this be good?

A question sentence is formed to get your attention and a response is expected. However, the toy does not care if the toddler answers or not. Is this an example of one-way communication or a social interaction? It is a one-way communication, a pseudo-conversation that in the end encourages more self-involvement and object-people confusion.

Why do we want to confuse our toddlers with this deception? Will the child learn to imitate the machine? If the child has a tendency toward ASD, he might. Talking toys can get the toddler's attention, engage in developmentally interesting displays, but in the final analysis will lead the toddler away from social interaction and towards self-involvement.

Just the other day, I saw an article about a new toy especially designed for children with ASD. Based on its description, I gathered the toy interacted with the child with movements and sounds, trying to simulate something alive. I am sure some children with ASD would find the object fascinating. But this is exactly the wrong thing such a child needs. There is no substitute for real beings in learning social interactions.

Corresponding to the period of time the incidence of ASD has skyrocketed, the sales of talking toys have skyrocketed, too. Could there be a connection?

Infancy Before Television and Video

What was life like before all these video devices? In this country, we have had television for some sixty years or so. The personal computer is about 35 years old. The internet really goes back no further than fifteen years. Smart phones became popular four years ago. Screens, screens, and more screens. As a physician, I spend a lot of time face-to-face with my patients but the rest of my day is one screen after another. But what was life like before all this video input? Has all this video become a part of the lives of our youngest children? What was life like for infants before television? What did families do together before television?

I do not have well-studied answers to these questions but I have asked my older patients about life before television. The first question I asked was whether they were bored. They chuckle and say no, not at all. I do not know what exactly to make of the chuckle but I suspect children were a little more mischievous back then as they invented activities to do.

Babies and children were the most entertaining things around for most families. They must have been the focus of a lot of attention. There was a lot of visiting between friends and families with babies tagging along for the general admiration.

People got together more in general, spending time in social clubs, playing cards or sports informally, going to local bars and similar activities. It seems to me the art of telling a joke or a good story was more widespread and more prized in my parent's generation than in mine.

You can read about family get-togethers that featured different family members singing, playing the piano, games, talent shows, etc. Today it seems the entertainment at family get-togethers is dominated by some major league sporting event shown on television. These old kinds of get-togethers seem curiously quaint now, almost bizarre. In short, before television, there was more social interaction and less passive television watching.

But what were babies and infants exposed to back then? They were usually exposed to an endless parade of faces and voices talking to them, smiling at them, picking them up and so forth. Everyone would try to make them smile or giggle. The fundamental currency, the fundamental nourishment of our social networks is mutual attention. I imagine babies got plenty of that.

Furthermore, I suppose the hopes and the fears of the mother and family were wrapped up in the little newborn. And for how long has infancy been like that in humans? I do not have the answer but it is very hard for me to imagine that it could have been very different since the start of our species. Then television appears and everything changes. This is a change of the culture of almost the entire planet, one that involves a shift in ideas, attitudes, appetites, habits and thoughts. It is one that affects everyday life in an incredibly pervasive way.

Introduction of Television and Video into the Lives of Infants

Television was first invented in 1927 in San Francisco by a 21 year old inventor. In 1939 RCA began broadcasting regular programs to a very small audience. By 1949 famous early television shows were being broadcast. I remember watching Captain Kangaroo as a child in the early 1950's. That show premiered in 1947.

The number of television sets in the United States grew from 6,000 in 1946 to 12 million by 1951. By 1955 half the households in the country had a television. In 1964, color was introduced. Cable TV was started in 1960 but in 1971 all of New York City had no more than 80,000 subscribers.

During the 1970's many more cable stations were added. In the 1980's the VCR became widely available and video games were introduced. In the 1990's the growth of cable television exploded, multiplying the number of channels available to most families.

In the late 1990's, television shows for infants and videos such as *Baby Einstein* and *Teletubbies* were introduced. Television now extends to all the corners of the world with over half the world's population having access to television. People watch an average of 2 ½ hours of TV a day, making it the activity that takes up most of the world's leisure time.

In this book, I have argued that the critical time for the infant to learn social communication and thereby assume their proper social role in their family, is during the first year of life. Are television and infant videos affecting this vital process, thereby causing the increasing incidence of ASD over the past 50 years?

If it is indeed true that television and video are causing ASD to increase over the past 50 years then we would expect to find:

1) Infants are increasingly exposed to television and video.
2) Infants actually pay attention to television and video.
3) Infants do not learn social communication from television or video.
4) Infants who watch video and television become more self-involved. Videos that are watched over and over again make this affect worse.
5) The increase in the incidence of ASD parallels the increase in exposure to television and video.

Exposure to Television and Video

The first statement is clearly true. There has been a sea of change in the television experience of infants between the times when the incidence of ASD was measured in children as 1-4 per 10,000 to today when one out of seventy boys has this problem. Fifty years ago television was still very new; the screen was black and white and quite small compared to now. The experience of TV viewing was quite different than today.

The first survey of the time infants spend watching TV is from the early 1990's. At that time parents reported that only 17% their infants watched any television at all. Among one year old toddlers, only 48% watched television and a mere 27% watched 1-2 hours per day.

By 2003, parents were again surveyed regarding the time their babies and toddlers spent viewing TV. The number of infants who watched TV increased dramatically from 17% to 52%. The overall average of number of hours infants and toddlers viewed television in this survey was about 2 hours per day. Considering infants are awake maybe eight hours a day, they were being exposed to TV during 25% of their time awake. If a toddler is enrolled in a home-based daycare, add to that average another 1 to 2 hours per day.

Of course, in many families the television is on all the time and is in the same room as the infant. Television was initially considered a luxury and a novelty. Those families lucky enough to be able to afford a television would have only one and the whole family would share that one TV. This in its way encouraged some social activity as the family members disputed which show would be the next to be watched.

Today families often have a television for each room in the house, including at times the bathroom. The screen size has increased dramatically as well. The sound systems are likewise very different from even 20 years ago. Home theaters are common, with sounds coming to the infants in such a room from all directions. All these features undoubtedly make the television experience more interesting and compelling to adults. They do the same for toddlers and infants.

The cultural expectation for infant television watching has changed dramatically. The importance of infant and toddler learning was discovered in the 1990's. The media companies took advantage of publicity surrounding these discoveries to create and sell a new product aimed at infants, the so called *edu-tainment* video.

These videos were sold to enhance learning during this sensitive period, to create little Mozarts and Einsteins. These claims do not hold up under scrutiny and were later retracted in the United States by *Baby Einstein.* However, the market was created and continues as a big business with parents of infants spending hundreds of millions of dollars on these videos each year.

So there are at least two factors contributing to the growth in exposures to TV in infancy over the past 50 years. The first is the increased presence of TV in families' life with more televisions per household, larger and brighter screens, and better audio. This has been a gradual but relentless process since the introduction of TV in the 1950's. The second is the deliberate marketing to parents of infants of videos and television series which started in the 1990's.

Infant Attention to Television and Video

In 2003, the official *Teletubbies* website in the United States suggested there is no reason why babies and toddler should not watch television since they enjoy it. That statement almost answers the second question: Does television capture the attention and interest of infants? It absolutely does.

There are three stages to the development of attention in infants. The first is present as early as birth. They orient towards objects and faces of interest. As they get a little older, they develop object and people recognition. The characteristic features of an object are put together to define what an object is or who a person is. This is thought to occur between 3 and 9 months of life. Later, but also during the first year of life, they develop sustained attention.

Sustained attention is characterized by a longer duration of attention, a characteristic facial expression (furrowed eyebrow and lips pursed open), and a slowing of the heart rate. Learning and memory is enhanced during periods of sustained attention and the threshold for distraction is higher. Let's call this 'concentration'. An infant at 3 months of age may have periods of sustained attention lasting 10 seconds while in a 2-year-old these periods may last several minutes or more.

To a baby or an infant, the colors, the movement, and the sounds seen on TV automatically attract attention. Babies are born with the ability to hear, to see color, and to recognize motion. During the first few months of life their visual system matures and by six months of life they have depth perception as well.

When babies are studied as they observe TV, the changes in color, motion, and sounds are all features attracting their attention. This is referred to as background television. It will capture the baby's attention repeatedly, but will not necessarily hold their attention. For a young infant, the video screen acts like a colorful kaleidoscope with a vocal and musical accompaniment. It is likely the most interesting thing the young infants are seeing and hearing in the nursery.

Background television is a distraction for infants and toddlers engaged in other activities such as playing with toys. The infant must choose which object in their environment to pay sustained attention to, the TV or the toy. Background television is a potent attractor of babies' attention. In this sense, it displaces visual attention from things the baby might explore by touch and manipulation. Remember, whatever a baby is looking at is what their brain is thinking about. TV is replacing active interactions with toys with passive TV viewing. Are infant videos creating baby Einsteins or baby couch potatoes?

It likely displaces attention away from two-way social interactions as well, but in the course of researching this book, I found no indication this likely and important phenomenon has been studied at all.

Starting as early as 3 month of age, infants demonstrate sustained attention while watching videos and television. Forty percent of infants start watching videos by six months of age. When watching these videos they show the same pattern of attention that adults show when watching television, with many periods of brief looking and fewer but longer periods of sustained attention.

At six months of age, the infant may start understanding the content, especially of videos that are viewed over and over again. The content is the meaning of the images and sounds projected by the video device. The content, as much as the infant grasps, serves to holds the infant's attention as well. After all, if the videos did not hold the infant's attention, no one would buy them. Once the infant's attention is captured, there is a certain inertia that keeps them focused on the screen, even if the content changes or becomes meaningless. They get 'zoned out' watching TV, just like adults.

Social Interaction and Television and Video

I hope we all agree social interaction and communication are central to human existence and the first year of life is the critical time for establishing the connection between the infant and the social networks around him. Could television and video help in this process? Could television be a window unto the world that infants could use to learn how social interaction operates? Could this kind of learning transfer to the family social network and facilitate the formation and growth of family relationships?

For older children and adults, television can truly operate like a window unto the world. They understand the image presented on the screen is quite different from actual experience of life. In some ways it is enhanced, and in other ways it is constricted. For infants this understanding is likely impossible.

Adults understand the content and images were created by a living person with intentions. They understand you cannot form a social relationship with that person unless you live in Hollywood. That understanding informs their television viewing experience. For infants and toddlers this understanding must be quite impossible.

The images of people on television must be confusing to infants. The images look, talk and act like humans but no conversation or interaction is possible. The images do not smile back or react to you. In this sense, they behave like objects. The images are some ambiguous experience for the infant. They appear to be alive, while really being mere illusions created on the video screen. These images cannot help infants with a tendency towards to ASD understand the real and very important difference between people and objects.

What is this distinction so important? An object has no feelings and there is no call for learning empathy and no activation of the social brain needed. People are the opposite. It is a critical distinction.

It is clear from studies infants cannot learn to speak a language simply by watching people talk on television. It is unlikely infants can learn social interaction skills in this way either. But, as far I can tell, it has not been studied. Certainly no participatory learning of social interactions is possible, since TV viewing is purely one-way communication.

I imagine learning how to be a part of a conversation for infants and toddlers is like you or I learning how to play the piano. We could watch lessons about piano playing on television for years and get nowhere.

Until we start taking lessons with a live teacher and our hands press real piano keys, we can never really learn how to actually play.

Self-Involvement and Television and Video

Today's infants are spending a good part of their days watching television. They hear language spoken and see facial expressions and body language on the video screen. To the best of their abilities, they pay attention to the content of the television shows or videos. We know the first year of life is extremely important for language acquisition. Just as infants are born ready to recognize faces, infants over 6 months old or so are ready to learn the sounds of language.

This must be a strong motivating force for infants. At this age, they are searching their environment for the spoken sounds around them. As discussed earlier, this is also the period of Motherese and baby talk. The learning of language helps cement the bond of affection of the baby to their mother and family.

Now suppose the infant is exposed to a television show or video either producing the sounds that mimic Motherese or something even more attention-catching. There is pleasure in this experience for the infant. Might this pleasure cause the baby to bond to the television show or video in some real way?

The process of language acquisition was always tightly linked to the infant's family before the advent of television. Bonding to a video or a television show is a form of self-involvement and social isolation. Television videos for infants are not played just once but many many times. Like hearing a certain song over and over again, the bonding and affection to this experience can grow over time and with repetition.

This bond ultimately strengthens self-communication and self-involvement, both of which are responsible for the development of ASD. Unfortunately, once again, I found no evidence in my research that this potentially important phenomenon of bonding to television and video has been studied at all.

It always seemed to me Otto's best friends were the talking cars he saw in the videos he watched over and over again. I can picture him when he was an infant watching a video image, which is a kind of object, of a car, another kind of object, acting just like a human. The car had a face with eyes and a mouth. It could talk and had facial expressions just like a living person. No wonder children exposed to videos like this develop object-person confusion. I think Otto felt himself to be more a part of the world of *Cars* than the world of living people who surrounded him.

Does Television Cause Autism?

Has the number of children with autism increased at the same time as the exposure to television and video to infants increased? The answer is clearly yes. California and Pennsylvania have kept track of the number of children who require special services because of developmental disabilities, including autism, since 1970. The numbers of cases were quite low back then.

Television channels exclusively for children were introduced in the late 1970s and early 1980s. By 1980 the number of children developing autism had increased by 30%. Rapid growth in households with cable television started in the 1980s. The rate of children developing autism doubled by 1986 and doubled again by 1992. The number of households with cable television likewise doubled in the early 1980's, and then doubled again 6 years later.

All these factors would have increased child and infant exposure to television and video at the same time the number of children with ASD was dramatically increasing. With the late 1990's came baby videos such as *Baby Einstein* and TV series such as *Teletubbies*, which increased television watching by infants dramatically. At the same time, the number of children with ASD continued its sharply upward progress.

I am not the first person to consider that television is a factor in the rapidly increasing incidence of ASD in today's society. In 2006, an landmark paper with the title "Does Television Cause Autism?" by Michael Waldman, Sean Nicholson, and Nodir Adilov was published on this very subject.

The research was done using two indirect measurements of television watching. It is well known that families watch more television when it rains or snows; it is the preferred indoor activity, or should I say inactivity, for families in the United States. The other factor was the introduction of cable television from 1972 to 1989 to different counties in California, Oregon, and Washington.

The study looked at television exposure during the first three years of life and the subsequent development of autism. The data was carefully analyzed. The study showed in those areas where the weather confined more people indoors and thereby causing them to watch more TV, the number of children developing autism increased by almost **40%**. The introduction of cable TV similarly increased the number of children developing autism by **17%**. These are astonishingly strong associations. They point the finger at television exposure as causing the increasing number of children with ASD.

Why has this very important study not garnered more attention? It should have triggered an avalanche of academic activity like the early twin studies of autism did. Instead, the author was met by scorn and ridicule. I suppose this is the risk of being the messenger of a message a culture does not want to hear and is not ready to listen to. Someday when this scourge of ASD has ended, parents around the world will have a lot to thank Dr. Waldman and his colleagues for.

That said, I think there are three reasons the study did not get the attention it deserved. The first is the study was done by economists using the tools that academic economists usually use to study financial matters. Other economists, who could have reviewed and analyzed the study, are naturally more interested in economic questions than ASD.

The academic psychologists, who have a real interest in ASD, were not familiar enough with the techniques the economists used in this study to really evaluate it. The third factor is this study relies on looking at events that occurred in a specific period of time, a sort of natural experiment that cannot be repeated. It makes the study virtually impossible to replicate. My opinion, as neither an academic psychologist nor an academic economist, is this study is very important. It is the smoking gun which shows the role of television as the cause of the increasing prevalence of ASD.

Dr. Waldman's landmark study provided an excellent indirect measurement of television watching in infancy. There is a more recent study that directly looks at the television viewing habits of infants and their subsequent development of ASD. It is a study from Bangkok, Thailand by Dr. W. Chonchaiya and her colleagues. That this study comes from Thailand serves as a reminder that ASD is a worldwide pandemic.

The author compares three groups of about 50 children each. The children in the first group have ASD. The children in the second group have delayed language development but are socially normal. The third group, the control group, has children without any of these problems, normal typical kids.

The author interviewed the parents about the infancy of their children. ASD begins in infancy so it is very good investigators are taking an interest in what happens during this key time in life.

The author questioned the parents about the age the child started watching television and how many hours a day the child watched television as an infant. The parents were also asked how many hours a day they had spent together with their infants.

Is it a surprise the children who later developed ASD not only watched television the earliest but also watched for the most hours?

The first principle a new parent learns is never disturb a sleeping or quiet baby. A baby needs so many hours of sleep, something like 16 hours a day. The rest of the day is either spent with company or by himself. If the baby is awake and quiet, he is generally not disturbed.

So imagine a baby is exposed to television at 6 months of age and he likes it. He finds it soothing and interesting. He is quiet in the presence of the television, especially when a familiar video is playing. He pays attention to the television and like most adults he may find lounging in the presence of undemanding one-way communication quite pleasant. He may even fuss and become irritable when the television is turned off.

In this situation the caregiver will naturally leave the television on more and more. And if the caretaker believes television and video watching are magically transforming their baby into a baby Einstein or Mozart, then why would the caregiver possibly turn the television off?

So you might expect the earlier the infant starts watching television, the more television he will end up watching. And it follows the more time he spends with television, the less time he will have to spend interacting with his caregivers.

The time the infant is in front of the television is time lost from learning how to participate in an enduring social relationship. That time could have actually been used to engage in two-way communication with repeated episodes of joint attention between the caregiver and the infant. This time is a kind of isolation, in a way similar to the poor baby monkeys that I talked about in Chapter 6 who could passively observe but did not get to participate in the social world around them.

The study showed that infants who later developed ASD, started watching television 6 months earlier, at 6 months of age, and ended up watching more than twice as much television per day compared to the control group of typically developing children. Not surprisingly, watching that much television left less time for actual social interactions with their caregivers. The children with ASD spent half as much time engaged in two-way communication with their caregivers as the children in the control group.

While this is just one study, the implication is clear. A parent, who turns on the television in front of a six month baby with a tendency towards ASD, is heading down a slippery slope. They may very well end up with a child with ASD, an event that could have easily been avoided.

Conclusion- The Role of Television and Video

I remember talking to a fellow physician from India many years ago and asking why poor people in India have so many children. He answered, "Because they do not have television." At the time I thought that was a pretty odd answer. I think I understand it now. Children were the best source of entertainment for the family until television came around. The business of life revolved around family and children.

Today many people today find their children are an unruly distraction from the pleasing electronic world of multiple video screens that follows us from work to home and back. It is known the incidence of ASD in the last twenty years has increased more in locales rich in the industries of advanced technology such as the Silicon Valley in California and a similar area in Holland.

It is also known the frequency of ASD increases with mothers who have delayed childbirth until their 40s. I am speculating, but is it possible these older mothers have more economic resources? Would they want to buy their children every kind of toy and form of infant edu-tainment they could afford? Would their houses be equipped with home theaters and snazzy computers with big screens? Would they have smart phones they could slip into the little hands of their children to get them to settle down a bit?

These dramatic changes in child care in the first year of life are causing two problems, both leading to the increasing prevalence of ASD. The first is the increasing exposure to infants to interesting objects and toys.

Picture for a minute a baby in a room with a picture of a man on the wall. How long would the picture hold the interest of the baby? I would say not long; A moment or two perhaps. Which is going to be more interesting to the baby: mom's face or the picture? No contest, mom. Give the picture lots of bright colors. Which is more interesting now: mom or the picture? Maybe if it is the first time the baby is seeing the picture, the picture may win for a few seconds, but after that mom. Keep on making the picture more and more interesting to the baby with colors, voices, sound effects, music, cartoon faces, motion, action, lights, and pretty soon, mom fades into the background.

As mom fades into the background, so goes all those opportunities for joint attention. After all, television is designed to get and keep our attention. Mom is designed to be a mother, to open the door to social communication and interaction. At some point, the picture wins. Mom's face is boring compared to the television screen.

If you are a baby boy who for genetic reasons finds social communication difficult, confusing, or uninteresting, whose company will be preferred? The television's, sadly enough. Some babies will prefer to be entertained in this private world rather than the pleasure of their caregiver's loving attention something a baby girl is more likely to desire.

As the infant gets a little older, 6 months or so, a second factor comes into play. This is one-way communication. Babies today are exposed to an endless and varied parade of faces and voices on video devices. What is the difference if these stimuli come from screens or live, face-to-face? The difference is fundamental, important and so simple. This is the key to understanding ASD and why there are so many more children are affected by this disorder today than ever before.

One-way communication is essentially **self-communication**, especially for an infant or toddler. It is a private conversation the child has with himself. The infant gladly pays attention to the faces and voices coming to him from different video devices including television. They are genetically prepared to pay attention to these types of stimuli. But they get no feedback, no reaction and no attention from the television screen, do they? So have they crossed the border from their own consciousness into another being's awareness? Is there any eye contact? Are there any episodes of joint attention? No, No, and No, obviously. These experiences are social dead ends.

These kinds of experiences if pleasurable will only lead to more self-involvement. Infants can never have a real social relationship with the people or characters shown on television. They can learn to imitate the sounds of language but without being connected in a conversation taking place in real time and in a familiar social setting, language is just voice. It has no meaning. Until a child is actively seeking attention from their family and has started to master language, one-way communication is a dangerous distraction from these most essential tasks of early childhood.

At 18 months toddlers start to understand the content of television and video much better than they did when they were younger. This is the time they really start to master understanding language. It is known this is also the very same age a group of children who had been apparently developing normally regress into ASD. These children stop talking and interacting with the adults around them. Could the content of television be the Pied Pipers of Autism for toddlers at this age?

When objects such as televisions, smart phones, computers, video games, etc. start to capture the attention of infants and children, some may abandon whatever social skills and interests they have previously acquired. This is the other side of brain plasticity. Without practice, we lose mastery of skills we have previously acquired.

This kind of thing can happen at any age really. When this happens in very young children such as infants and toddlers, they can develop ASD. If they are five or six years old, they may develop ADHD (Attention Deficit Hyperactivity Disorder), another form of social disruption, in some ways quite similar to ASD.

I remember when I was young teen ager and discovered the library would let me take out as many books as I wished. I went on a reading feast. I lost interest in my family and friends who seemed less interesting and less real to me than the characters in the books I was reading. Today, the forms of one-way communication are more compelling than when I was that age. I suspect more people now, especially men, find more pleasure in one-way communication as opposed to social relationships, than ever before in the history of mankind.

Conclusion- The Role of Toys

Are toys affecting our babies the same way as television is? Baby toys, and for that matter, children's toys have changed a lot in the last fifty years. While I have not seen any crib toys with actual video screens yet, I cannot imagine they are far away. Perhaps they might even come equipped with a camera so a parent could watch their baby in the crib while they are away at work or shopping.

This would be the perfect item for the busy multitasking parent of today. The device would of course educate and entertain the baby at the same time. It could even be a phone app so that during a business meeting the parent could check up on their baby; maybe the screen could project the parent's picture to the baby at the same time for the baby's amusement and comfort. As I say this, one side of me is shuddering thinking about how much babies need face-to-face communication and the other side is saying: what a cool idea for a working parent, which seems to be almost all parents these days.

But really, what about toys? How do toys fit in the ASD picture? Do they encourage social communication or self-communication? The first aspect to consider is whether the toy is designed to be played together with the caregiver or not. If the toy was designed for both to play with together, then it would encourage social communication through joint attention.

I did a little informal research on this topic myself. Surfing the internet, I found a catalog of toys from *Fischer Price*. Looking at the toys for infants, I saw just one toy illustrated with a picture of mother and baby at play together. The rest just had pictures of babies playing with the toys alone.

The toys for infants were brightly colored and often placed around the baby so wherever he happened to look he would see some brightly colored, often moving object, and sometimes even a mirror. Babies like looking at mirrors. They like seeing faces. But looking at your own face in a mirror does not encourage back and forth social interaction, does it?

The crib toys were festooned all over and around the crib. A mother approaching the baby in such a crib would be almost completely hidden from the baby by the multitude of crib toys. Infant toys are designed to get and hold the baby's attention. They are attention grabbers. They are designed to keep the baby quietly amused. The more attention the toy (an object) gets the less that is available for the baby's caregivers.

Again, the same problem holds forth as with video screens. At some point, they are more interesting to the baby than the mother. The baby's attention and focus moves from a loving, living, interacting person to an object. This is especially an issue for the babies who for genetic reasons are more vulnerable to have problems with social communication. Why struggle to learn to communicate with your mother and family when you are very well amused by yourself?

Please remember these changes in toys are not only a radical departure from how infants have been raised for eons but also a recent one. One hundred years ago or even fifty years ago the best entertainment a baby had was his immediate family and the most entertaining thing in the household was the baby.

In my opinion, together television, video screens and infant toys are *the* environmental cause of the surge in the prevalence of ASD in modern culture. They are the Pied Pipers of Autism. That is the essence of the Integrated Theory of Autism. With all these children being affected by ASD, a virtually new industry has arisen to help these children emerge from the social isolation of ASD. In the next chapter, I will briefly talk about some programs that have had success and what that says about the nature of ASD.

Chapter Eight
Treatment

What can be done to help children who have been affected by ASD? Are they condemned to a life of social isolation and narrow self-interests? Can they ever learn how to make the social connections they need to make new friends, to be a part of the social world around them, and to achieve independence? These are questions I hear from parents of children with ASD.

As I have discussed in Chapter Two, there are two groups of symptoms and findings in ASD. The first group is related to difficulties in social communication and interaction, and the second group is related to excessive self-involvement and self-stimulation. Restricted interests, repetitive motions, over- and under- sensitivity to different sensations, and the act of repeating sounds and words are some of the symptoms in this second group. These are all symptoms of a child living in a private world of self-involvement. Even the name of the condition, 'autism,' which was coined in 1910 from the Greek word 'autos', refers to self-involvement.

My theory of autism, The Integrated Theory of Autism, states that children are born with a genetically determined blend of interest in social communication and self-involvement. Some children are by nature, more introverted, others more extroverted. As they go through life, experiences will push infants and children one way or another on this spectrum. Lots of time and affection from an attentive caregiver pushes them towards liking social interactions. Exposure to fascinating objects such as The Pied Pipers of Autism pushes them towards self-involvement and away from empathetic relationships with other people.

This second type of exposure needs to be changed. While 100,000s of children have already developed ASD, the good news is certain types of treatment have been found to be effective for older children well past the critical age for learning social communication. In this chapter, I will discuss these treatment programs, all of which have ways of opening the door to social development for these children. As social interactions improve, the symptoms of excessive self-involvement recede.

Studying Treatment Programs for ASD

While it is true that the 'critical period' for learning social communication is during the first and second year of life, nevertheless a great deal of success has been reported in helping children with ASD emerge from social isolation later in life. This process of learning involves 'brain plasticity' and as such is much more difficult than during infancy. There are few well-done controlled trials of any of the myriad of different therapeutic programs offered to the parents of the child with ASD.

The difficulty of doing a controlled trial with this condition is clear. The methods used in any of the treatments are more complex than simply administering a medication. A pill may calm down a child with ASD. But it is not surprising no pill can provoke a child's interest in social communication or teach a child how to find pleasure in their relationships with other people.

A good study requires a balanced control group. The interventions involved in any of these programs are complicated and so long-lasting that setting up a control group is fraught with difficulty. The programs are often led by a charismatic leader, someone with a special feeling for children with ASD. Charisma is hard to measure, harder to reproduce, but may be an important factor in the success or failure of any program.

Furthermore, a good study should also be blinded; that is the experimenter and the subject should not know who received what intervention. In this area, blinding the experimenter is practically impossible and blinding the subject is frankly impossible. The subjects will know what treatment they have received and it would be difficult for the experimenter not to figure it out as well.

The process of healing takes place over a period of years and our measurements of degrees of healing of ASD are not well-validated. Each program has its own outlook on what is a successful outcome. Some programs emphasize the child's ability to fit in and manage themselves in a certain social setting such as school. Others look more at the ability to connect with other people, make friends, and the like.

The programs all take time and effort by other people, which is hard to standardize, unlike the milligrams in a pill, so the intervention is hard to measure and quantify. The interventions likewise require the formation of new social relationships, which also is not simply studied in a laboratory. Although difficult to measure and assess, observations have shown some children with ASD are getting better in certain programs on a regular basis.

After the age of seven or eight, some children with ASD will improve and gradually appear more neurotypical. Whether they develop strategies linked to their cognitive abilities and use these to get around their more fundamental social problems or whether they gradually learn to communicate empathetically remains to be seen. However, some improvement can happen after this age with or without participation in any particular program.

In the next part of this chapter I will discuss some of the obstacles programs for children with ASD face and then three programs that have reported success in the face of these obstacles; what these programs share and how they differ. In line with the overarching theme of this book, my focus will be in how these programs help children with ASD learn how to participate in empathetic two-way communication.

Obstacles to Treatment- Low Cognitive Ability

It is important to keep in mind that a child with ASD has special difficulties learning. Once the door to social communication and relationships is partially or fully closed, learning (outside the narrow self-interests of the child) becomes much more challenging. These issues are in addition to the handicap of a low level of cognitive ability (IQ) which is often found in low-functioning children with ASD. Fortunately, most of the children with mild ASD have normal or even high cognitive abilities. The children with ASD and a low level of cognitive ability face difficulties beyond the scope of this book. However it is important to keep in mind that the assessment of cognitive ability in a child with ASD has special challenges and is fraught with difficulties.

Obstacles to Treatment- Learning After the Critical Period

My critical period for learning languages has long since passed. Nevertheless, I am interested in learning Portuguese since my wife's family is from Brazil. To learn this new language, I have to start with the basics. It won't do to watch a Brazilian soap opera on television in the beginning; I would not understand a word that was spoken. I have to learn one word at a time. I need two-way communication with someone who is willing to patiently help me by correcting my errors and mispronunciations.

My brain has to learn to distinguish the sounds of the new language. I have to focus and really play attention to make sense of what at first sounds like gibberish to me. It is difficult to acquire proficiency in a new language. Compare that with infants who after 12 months of age have effortlessly finished learning how to identify all the sounds of the language they will use with their family.

It is not easy for me to learn Portuguese, and if I was not motivated by my wife's encouragement, I would have given up long ago. I am gradually improving, but I know that no one will ever mistake me for a native speaker. With time, effort, interest and practice my brain will acquire a working knowledge of Portuguese, but my critical period for learning a new language has long passed. Whatever plasticity my brain has will not stretch that far.

Likewise, the child with ASD can acquire interest and skills in social communication, but they are not likely to be at the same level as a child who acquires this capability during the first and second years of life and spends the rest of his life practicing it, day after day. The challenge is to learn enough to form and find trustworthy friendships and relationships.

If we agree the critical period to learn social communication is during the 1st and 2nd years of life, then what are we to do to help these children to acquire social communication after this age? This is the fundamental challenge for all programs for ASD.

Obstacles to Treatment- Interest and Motivation

The first problems any program for children with ASD needs to address are interest and motivation. The program must capture the child's attention. Let us face it, children with ASD have others things they would rather be doing than socialize. Learning social communication in the end must come through social communication.

If a person with ASD has no interest in socializing how will he learn this? Putting an unmotivated child with ASD in front of a computer screen with lessons in social behavior and hoping he learns this skill from a video is most likely going to fail. Ultimately both motivation and practice with real people in real time is required to learn these skills.

The most difficult issue initially facing a program for ASD is establishing a positive channel for social interaction, the same challenge a caretaker faces with a newborn. Gradually two-way communication must somehow become more interesting and rewarding than one-way communication and self-stimulation, at least during the part of the day in which this learning will take place.

Distracting objects such as television, videos, computers or talking toys all focus the child's attention and pleasure towards self-communication. They need to be avoided entirely or at the least used very judiciously in any program. The rewards of social communication must replace, or at least supplement, the pleasures of self-communication and self-involvement.

Obstacles to Treatment- Imitation, Joint Attention and Relationships

Most of what we learn to do, as children, comes from imitation. We are born into a small social network, our family, and we spend years observing and trying to be just like them. The way we walk, talk, move, speak, listen, and eat is formed and shaped by observing the people in our family.

Children with ASD often have great difficulties with imitation of other people. Their interest and attention is focused on objects or things, and *not* human relationships. They do not understand what makes other humans, including their teachers, tick and may not have the interest to even observe let alone emulate them. So in a school setting, learning by imitation of their teachers is severely impaired.

People including teachers seem to be more like objects to a child with ASD, something the rest of us can barely imagine or picture. He may find the feelings and intentions of other people are more or less undecipherable. Without any good idea of their intentions, he may find teachers' behavior baffling, unpredictable, and disturbing.

A child with ASD comes to school more or less in his own world connected more to some video experience than to the people surrounding him. How then will he connect to his teacher? Joint attention is the basis for people connecting to each other. A child with ASD needs to find these kinds of experiences with other people if a program is to help him emerge from social isolation.

The conduct of any school program depends on the formation of relationships between teachers and students and likewise between students and each other. Students need to figure out where to go, when to go there, and how to behave. They do that by being with other students. Children with ASD almost by definition have great difficulty forming these relationships and making these connections. To get around this problem programs for ASD are often set up with rigid fixed schedules.

Expressive social skills such as conversation are learned via imitation as children form relationships with other people. A successful program for children with ASD must in the end imparts these social skills. The problem for these programs is then how to help a child with ASD make social connections.

Trying to form a relationship with a child with ASD has its challenges and frustrations for the teacher. Unlike normotypical children, a child with ASD will often not welcome attention. Even a high-functioning talkative child with Asperger's will not show the empathetic instantaneous reactions that so characterize conversation. Without two-way communication coming from the student the teacher may find working with a child with ASD is in the end tedious and unrewarding. So an additional challenge for these programs is maintaining their teachers' interest and motivation.

Obstacles to Treatment– Shaping Behavior with Rewards

Another way we learn is through rewards and punishments. This also has its challenges for children with ASD. With a normotypical child or adult their rewards and punishments can come simply from either the approval or disapproval of the people who matter to them.

For instance, when I sing I notice everyone leaving the room (except my little girl, who actually likes to hear me sing). This gives me notice that whatever skills it takes to be a singer in public, I do not have. Listening to myself sing alone, I might not have figured this out. On the other hand, if the people I care about all came up to me and told me I had a beautiful voice, then I might be encouraged to take lessons, join a choir, and, who knows, even record my voice.

Rewards and punishments, such as praise and ridicule, given gently or not so gently by our social networks are how you and I navigate this social world we live in. A child with ASD is more or less cut off from these rewards and punishments. I think this is part of why raising a child with ASD is so stressful and difficult; all the normal things a parent does to shape a child's behavior simply do not work.

Any program for children for ASD has to have a system of rewards and at times punishments which encourage and reward learning. Rewards, once a social relationship is established, can come from the relationship. Before that food or other things the child likes can serve the same purpose.

I have said before the key thing for a child with ASD to learn is *social communication,* but he also needs to learn whatever knowledge and skills will be required to navigate his future life.

Trust is a very big issue for the establishment of social relationships. A program by its very nature is asking the child to join a new social network, outside of the family. This is a difficult step for children with ASD. Many times a child entering a program will already have had many painful and baffling social experiences with and away from his family. These experiences will lead to fear of even being in social settings, let alone joining and trusting a new social group.

Naturally this fear must be replaced by trust before learning can take place. This trust will be very difficult for a child with ASD to acquire. They usually have an underdeveloped 'theory of mind' or the ability to 'mind read' other people. Normotypic people use this ability to pick out which people in the world to trust or not. Without this ability, the only way trust can only be acquired is gradually over time with experience.

Punishment will not only be baffling to the child with ASD but will actually cause the child to further withdraw from social contact and thereby dash any hope of learning how to socialize. Any effective program must avoid punishments in order to allow the growth of trust.

As a child begins to develop social behavior and therapeutic relationships in a program, care must be taken to protect the child during this delicate period from negative social experiences such as teasing, bullying, and ridicule.

These principles are much like the way mothers treat their babies. Mothers do not punish their babies because not only would it be senseless but it undermines the development of trust. Mothers are also very vigilant to protect their babies from bad experiences with other people. And mothers are all about establishing a meaningful social connection with their babies.

Since rewards for the child with ASD cannot initially be social, some other impetus must be used. Again, following the cues of the mother-baby relationship, human social contact must be associated with pleasure and comfort. The pleasure could come from touch, food, or whatever pleases the child.

For the purposes of learning social communication, the rewards should not come from forms of one-way communication such as watching a favorite video, however enjoyable that may be for the child. This kind of reward runs the risk of the child taking two steps backwards for every step forward. It is like rewarding an alcoholic for a brief period of sobriety with a drink. This strategy may be possible but it has its obvious problems.

As the child improves they will likely need lessons and experiences sequenced like the normal pattern of social development (see Chapter 2) with social pretending, social imitation and friendship formation. Their social development will be out of step with their cognitive and physical development until they catch up with other children their age.

It was once thought ASD was a hopeless disorder. This was when there were fewer children with this disorder. Perhaps they were a different group of children with a stronger genetic component. At any rate, in the past these unfortunate children were often institutionalized which, as you might imagine, encouraged even more self-involvement and social isolation.

Despites these obstacles, the following three programs have shown children with ASD can and do improve with treatment. Just as environmental factors during the first two years of life can lead a child to ASD, an environmental factor such as one of three following programs for ASD can lead a child away from ASD.

Program One- Cross-Species Treatment

The first program I will discuss is cross-species therapy. Dogs and horses have lived with humans for a long time; they were social animals long before they became associated with our species. Over time a strong mutual bond with humans developed. This association was a big advantage to both the humans and to the animals.

Depending on the breed and training, these animals have the capability to establish empathetic relationships with humans. Dogs will actually interact with humans eye to eye. I am no student of dogs or horses, but I would say the animals might have a critical period early in life to develop this inherent capability.

While success has been reported with horses, dolphins, and dogs, allow me to focus on dogs for the remainder of this brief discussion. Dogs are the most practical animal to engage in a therapeutic relationship with a child with ASD. They are very sensitive to the social network they live in. They are used to living in a hierarchical social network and expect it when living with humans. Much like the feudal relationship between lord and vassal, they offer loyalty and devotion in exchange for resources such as food and shelter.

However, the dog does not always make a good social connection with a child with ASD. The dog may regard the child as having very little standing in the household, therefore not worthy of his attention. Furthermore, the child may be fearful of the dog. But sometimes a connection between the two can and will be established.

For the child with ASD, this represents a neat half step towards social communication. The dog can give unconditional attention without the burden of using human language. Dogs like to be touched, and touch is the simplest form of two-way communication. Dogs are almost implicitly trustworthy, something the child will learn over time.

The dog then becomes an emotional safe station for the child, often more so than other family members who may have difficulty letting go of the notion that the child should be more normal. The dog will accept and love the child just as he is. There are many reports of children bonding with dogs and establishing two-way communication even with eye contact. This relationship can serve as a bridge to subsequent human relationships.

Program Two- Applied Behavior Analysis

Another well-known program for children with ASD is Applied Behavior Analysis (ABA), based on work done by Ivar Lovaas at UCLA. The program has been working with people with ASD for many years. It is intensive and involves between twenty to forty hours a week of treatment. The therapist keeps extensive notes on their patients' progress. These notes have been useful in documenting the success of the program.

The principles come from operant conditioning, which is simply shaping behavior with rewards and punishments. They approach the patient as a collection of behaviors that need to be changed and expanded. They do not try to understand what is going on inside the child's mind which is fine. They use rewards, typically bits of food, to shape behavior. They break down the process of achieving the desired behavior in to small easy steps.

For instance, to teach a patient how to swallow pills, they would start out with a very small pill that could be easily swallowed. Then as success was achieved they would gradually increase the size of the pill until the required size was swallowed easily and reproducibly.

These lessons take place in a special location, free of distractions, either in the child's home or school. If any of the programs have been well studied and the improvements well documented, it is this program.

How does this program address the need to establish trust and social communication? The key is time and attention. The child and the teacher have a lot of time together: 20 to 40 hours a week. They certainly have more time than two busy parents would. The teacher, as a healer, feels they are doing an important job. They are truly professionals with special skills that have been acquired through diligent training and study. The relationship with the child is an important one for the teacher.

The setting is one with minimal distractions and the child gets the full attention of the teacher day after day. Both teacher and child then have the shared task and a common interest in the behaviors being worked on. This is an excellent environment for the child to re-establish social communication; the little interest the child with ASD has in learning social communication is given fertile soil to grow in. The teacher hopefully becomes a trusted friend and if the program is functioning properly, the child should look forward to the interaction. The development of trust and affection are the true markers of success in a program for children with ASD.

Program Three-Son-Rising ®

The third program I will discuss is the 'Son-Rising' ® program, also referred to as the Option Program. This program is quite different from the ABA program, and while it does not have the history and detailed records that are part of the ABA program, I find it very interesting.

It helped Otto and has won an award in the category for "Best Therapy" for children with ASD at an AutismOne conference. Good results have been reported with the use of the program.

Let us look at how this program establishes trust and social communication. Social communication begins with imitation of other humans; a baby will imitate the mother even during the first few months in life. The mirror neuron system, as discussed earlier in the book, exhibits how our brain is built especially for imitation.

For the baby, imitation of the caregiver is the bridge to intimacy and trust and the gateway to social relationships in general. The child with ASD has missed the critical stage for learning social communication. At the time the child with ASD enters this program, he is usually busy imitating sounds, bits of speech, videos and motions, but *not* other people.

The program encourages the parents to find enthusiastic and trainable volunteers as 'helpers'. The helper is encouraged to speak slowly and exaggerate facial expressions and vocal intonations. Again, does a mother not do the same thing with her own infant by speaking Motherese?

The program uses 'helpers' to interact with the child with ASD. This program has the very interesting idea that if the child will not imitate the helper, then the helper can at least imitate the child.

The helper has to develop a genuine interest in the *stims* of the child, or whatever interests the child has that can be *shared*. Consequently, these activities act as a bridge to establish social communication. The helper joins in the child's stims. These repetitive motions, so much a marker of the social isolations of the child with ASD, become a shared activity; one the child can hardly help joining in.

Through imitation, the helper demonstrates to the child that the child is already communicating and the helper is interested in understanding the child's heretofore private messages. The helper, of course, gives the child their full attention and the activities they share is any play the child likes that *they can do together*.

The point is this program makes it easy and interesting for the child to socialize. As in the ABA program, this takes time; typically 20 hours a week in a special setting where the helpers work or shall we say play with the child. The setting is free of decoration and certainly has no distracting televisions, video screens or fascinating toys. The space, free of distractions, makes the other person in the room, the helper, the most interesting thing around. Furthermore, the program pays special attention to establishing eye contact and joint attention.

Program Goals

Once interest, trust, and a channel of communication have been established, how do the programs manage learning and shaping behavior? Ultimately, the question revolves around what the goals are for these children. This is an important question.

The answer is tied to the needs and desires of the child. Hopefully, as the child improves, their needs and desires will be articulated and understood by their families and their close social networks. The child, just like any child, needs to be prepared for their future life as best as possible. How do these programs go about doing this task?

The ABA program has a simple approach to this issue: it is designed to shape behavior via a systematic delivery of rewards to the children as they acquire the desired skills and behaviors. The selection of the skills to be learned is individualized, and is appropriate for the developmental stage and past achievements of the child. With the proper set of behaviors and adequate support in place, the child may be able to return to the regular classroom as the start of a regular life.

A frequent criticism of this program is although behavior has been normalized and fits in with the culture, social communication and social relationships have not. The two-way communication the child has established with the teacher does not always generalize to other people in the child's social network.

The child's real need is to develop the skills to form new, trusting and affectionate relationships via social communication. In others words, can the child begin to understand and care about the gentle rewards and punishments we all get from our own social networks and use them to shape new behaviors in different settings? Can the child begin to understand and appreciate what makes other people in this world we live in tick? Can the child learn to tell whom he can trust?

The Son-Rise ® program has a different approach to this issue of goals. It clearly focuses on the establishment and development of social communication and has little use for special education programs with other children with ASD. It is easy to see why; putting a bunch of kids together who do not know how to communicate to start out with is an unlikely way to learn social behavior. Any imitation they do will be of other children's stims.

They also have little use for mainstreaming the child; in other words, putting the child into a regular classroom. Again, I think the point is well taken. The child will be very vulnerable to negative social experiences, such as teasing and ridicule, in this setting unless he is armed ahead of time with suitable defensive social skills. Negative experiences will tend to push the child towards more to self-involvement and the consolations provided by one-way communication.

So how is the child to develop the knowledge and behaviors they need to fit into their social networks and lead an independent adult life? The answer in this program is twofold. First, many of these children are quite bright. They easily learn to read with the right motivation. As they gain mastery of the tools of social communication, their interests will naturally broaden and become more normalized within their culture. Given their native intelligence and their ability to focus, they can rapidly acquire the abilities they need to build their life.

The second part is as they become more socially adept, they also become more tuned into the feelings of other people. In other words as they develop empathy, the rewards and punishments that shape the behavior of these children can come more naturally from the people around them. This is a lofty goal. This program is essentially saying that the primary focus and emphasis needs to be on repairing the defect on social interactions and the rest will come. This fits in well with the Integrated Theory of Autism.

Interestingly enough, as socialization improves the self-involvement symptoms of ASD seem to diminish as well. As the child emerges from the web of self-communication and can use joint attention to make sense of the physical and social world around them, these other symptoms often abate spontaneously. With the ABA program, the behavioral symptoms are the subject of training and teaching so they abate directly as the result of the programs teachings. Nevertheless, I would imagine other symptoms that are not directly being addressed would improve as well at the same time.

Otto

Author, Otto and Eric watching a video

My own interest in ASD really started with my nephew Otto. My wife and I were visiting Otto when he was about two years old. She noticed he did not like to be held and or play with other children. She also noticed when he was watching television you could walk between him and the television and he would act like you were merely an object blocking the way. Later on he was diagnosed with the Asperger's form of ASD. After failing to be helped by psychoanalysis, his mother selected the Son-Rise ® program. He has improved as the family has implemented the program as best as they could.

The Son-Rising ® program focuses on the development of social communication. As Otto's social abilities improved, his self-stimulation symptoms have likewise resolved without any attention to retraining any specific behavior or stim. For instance, my sister-in-law describes in a letter to me that he used to love to jump on a spoon again and again.

After some time in the program, he just lost interest in that stim and it was not replaced with any other repetitive motion activity.

Was this just coincidence or was it a change brought about by the program? That is hard to prove one way or the other. But to me, the program makes a lot of sense. Once a child redevelops an interest in social behaviors, they have to lose some of the focus on one-way communication and self-involvement. Oh, he still loves his computer and his videos but they are not his whole life, people fit in too.

She also wrote to me that once eye contact between them started, the sensitivity he had had to loud noises stopped. Undoubtedly with eye contact came the re-initiation of joint attention and social referencing.

Again, was it just a coincidence? People have a tendency to link cause and effect to events that are related in time. Nevertheless the chain of events is at least consistent with the idea that the self-involvement symptoms of ASD are truly secondary to the loss of social communication, not some nuero-genetic phenomenon.

The interesting thing for me about the ABA and Son-Rise ® programs is not their differences but their similarities. The two programs both make it very easy for the child to establish new relationships and open the door to two-way communication. Both programs establish trust gradually over time. Both programs have learned the importance of minimizing distractions especially from video devices. Both programs work with joint attention. Both programs involve a lot of time with the expectation of gradual improvement. There are significant differences between the programs but there is a lot of common ground as well.

Conclusion

The definitive study on the treatment of ASD has not been done by any means. The difficulty in studying the effectiveness of the different programs is obvious and hard to surmount. It is tough for a parent to pick out the best program for their child. I hope my comments are helpful to them. Meanwhile, there is a tremendous amount of money, time, and effort being spent on improving the quality of life for these children.

For the family, having a child with this condition is a huge problem, taking time and resources away from the rest of the family. Prevention is the ideal solution, and I think ridding the nursery of the Pied Pipers of Autism will go a long way in that direction.

Nevertheless, the problem of the best way to restore the ability of these children to be a part of their social networks or to 'social health' will remain very important.

The first thing needing to be done is to make a series of validated and developmentally appropriate measurements of social communication behavior in infants and young children. The chart that I created in Chapter 2 showing the normal development of social skills needs to refined and improved. These studies could be the basis of an instrument for measuring social development in children. Fortunately, this work is already underway in different centers for the study of ASD.

The Denver Development Scale is a scale used for looking at development in children in general. It looks at landmarks in development in different areas. For instance, there is the gross motor group, the fine motor group, and the language group. I would add a new group for social communication that would measure when a child acquires different social skills. Then all children could be tested for these skills at their regular checkups as the American Academy of Pediatrics already encourages. There is good reason to hope that the earlier ASD is detected the better the outcome will be for the child.

With the creation of a good measurement instrument for social development in this age group, treatment interventions could be evaluated with actual controlled studies. The studies could demonstrate the effect the different forms of one-way communication have on social development at as child grows up.

The best treatments might be found to be different for the child or adult with high-functioning Asperger's Syndrome (now called mild ASD) than the child with moderate ASD, who in turn is a world apart from a child with severe ASD with low-cognitive abilities.

People with mild ASD have language ability and are already engaged in a limited form of two-way communication. Their skills, interest and pleasure in social communication are underdeveloped. You could say their social brain has not formed as expected. They need to learn how to accurately assess the intentions and emotions of other people and to understand what makes other people tick.

As they become adults, they seem fully capable of making their own decisions regarding the need and desire for therapy. They may prefer to stay exactly as they are, comfortably alone, or they may want some services or coaching. While not easy, thanks to brain plasticity, they can improve their social communication skills with time, motivation and skilled helpers.

Often adolescence is a difficult time for people with ASD, as the hormonal changes drive them to want to join adolescent groups that may not really want to include them. Social rejection can lead to alienation, fear and anger.

Relationships can be difficult and uncomfortable for people with ASD. Maintaining a marriage is usually extremely difficult. Of course, judging by today's divorce rates, marriage is a challenge for anyone in our culture.

Outside of relations with other humans, their intense focus and their freedom from having their thoughts tied to the ideas of the existing culture at times allows them to make great creative achievements advancing our culture in general. But in general, they are left with a lonely life.

My personal opinion is that we should strive to make our children and ourselves more like Benjamin Franklin. He is, as you may have guessed, my personal favorite amongst the founding fathers of our country. He was a genius in both self and social communication, one-way and two-way communication. We should try to have it all, or better yet, have as much of both forms of communication as we are capable of having.

A world full of independent thinkers who are socially conscious and adept would be wonderful. Meanwhile, before utopia arrives, how can we prevent ASD with its excessive self-involvement? I will discuss my ideas on this important and pressing matter in the next chapter.

About Otto – Seven
Rosangela's Stories- Four

In February 2010 when we were chasing information about autism on the internet we found the Son-Rise© website. We registered to get some brochures and, as soon as we had those papers in our hand we started using some of their principles. The very first one we used was "joining the stims".

Otto used to take two spoons and jump on them all the time, everywhere, completely absorbed in that activity. When I first joined him it was in the kitchen (we didn´t have the playroom), after joining him for half an hour I introduced a variation, suggesting to him to invite those guys (the spoons) to jump on a moving rock (which was a moving plate) and then on a wicker basket of a hot air balloon (which was a colander). He liked the idea, and pretty soon those spoons started jumping on my objects. He allowed me to be part of his play.

Next day he invited me to play with him before he started his stim. Once I was part of his game I asked him "Who were they (the spoons)?" He replied: "They are Lilo and Stitch." [Characters from a Disney video and film]. Soon we were playing different games. I noticed his games were always a copy of some games he had played in the computer or scenes he had seen on TV. So I used these games/scenes as a tool to make him interact and play with me.

We got very excited about this initial result and thought about going to attend Son-Rise Startup. With the great support (in every sense) from my sister Roseli, I attended Son-Rise StartUp in June 2010 at the Autism Treatment Center of America in Sheffield, MA. I returned with a great excitement realizing how potentially powerful this treatment can be.

In August our playroom was all set up and I had 3 volunteers. We met and we discussed about our objectives: by prioritizing eye contact, joining stims and other kinds of games, in a 1:1 non-distracting environment, we wanted to improve in his behavior. We wanted to decrease his aggressiveness and hyperactivity. We wanted to increase the time he would spend in our world and to stimulate the use of "I" and "me" instead of "Otto". He used to speak in third person always saying, "Otto wants this..."

In the first playroom sessions he didn´t want to stay there, but soon he started loving that room and he would spend all day there. I played with Otto by myself in the beginning and I had some progress, but when I introduced the volunteers his progress was so much faster, it was like the volunteers had pushed a trigger and it was so evident that therapy was working.

Before the volunteers, with only with me playing with him, he improved from: never answering when we called his name when we were in front of him, to: yelling "I am here!" when we called his name even when he was in another room of the house. The first time I called from the kitchen "Dinner is ready!" and Otto answered from the living room "Coming." I cried!

With the volunteers, things were so good, games were funny, Otto was so happy. The difficulty was to hold back Erik who wished to be part of that fun too. He wanted to be in the playroom.

After 1 month with the volunteers, Otto increased his eye contact when we were talking to him but he wasn´t able to talk and look simultaneously. After 2 months he diminished the use of the trampoline and, we noticed he was less hyperactive. His aggressive behavior was also better.

Suddenly, in the end of September he regressed and spent two weeks with no eye contact. He refused to play with the volunteers. He spent those two weeks absorbed in his world just speaking to himself repeating the same words again and again. Since we knew it could happen, we just waited until he would be ready to continue.

When someone asked Samahria Kaufmann [from Son-Rise], in one of her interviews, why these "regressions" occur, she said: It´s like when you are climbing a mountain. After reaching a certain point with a lot of effort you just need to get some rest, so stopping for some time doesn´t mean you are going down. You are just preparing yourself for the next journey.

Even though Otto was unresponsive we continued with the sessions. One day when Tiago (one of the volunteers) entered in the playroom Otto came back from his "rest" and he spent 2 hours on a roll with Tiago staying 100% of the play time with him with full attention. We were amazed.

After 4 months his eye contact was great, he could look and talk for few seconds, he was less hyperactive, he would spend one hour playing with memory cards, or "cai não cai" or Monopoly (the one with Cars theme, of course). He was using "I," "me," "mine" etc... instead of his name. After five months, he would spend 10 to 20% of the time in his world and 80 to 90% with us out of the playroom. His eye contact lasts longer and he started playing with his brother.

He had regression other times. But always came back.

Today he makes eye contact even though not good as a neurotypical child. He can look and talk simultaneously, he interacts with people, he has friends at school and he plays with his brother most of the time when we are at home.

In January we did not continue Son Rise sessions because my husband's chemotherapy treatments were making everyone very tired. But we still keep the principles all the time, everywhere we are with kids.

- Rosangela Eichler 2012

Chapter Nine
Prevention and New Directions

This book has argued that ASD is a condition arising from genetic sources and from exposure to one-way communication. Exposure to The Pied Pipers of Autism has become a normal part of the first year of life for infants today. These changes in infant care practices have taken place in my lifetime during the same time ASD has gone from an exceedingly rare to a disturbingly common condition. The core idea behind *The Integrated Theory of Autism is exposure to one-way communication impacts social development adversely.* If the exposure happens early enough in life ASD may develop.

I have little doubt one-way communication in infancy is the major environment factor causing ASD. It seems to me the exposure to television, video devices and talking toys in infancy is *the environmental cause of the current worldwide pandemic of ASD.* At the very least it is a major contributing factor. Clearly more research and studies need to be done. Sooner or later those people who make the decisions of where research dollars are spent are going to have to start looking at social development and one-way communication.

In the chapter that follows I will make a number of suggestions to parents with infants and toddlers. Does a prudent new parent need to wait another 10 years until all the studies are done to make the changes I am suggesting? No. I am not proposing anything dangerous, like not vaccinating your children.

To the new parent, I am suggesting returning to some practices that once were the rule but are no longer widespread in our culture. These practices should, at the very least, lead to the development of stronger social bonds between your child and you and to the social networks you are both a part of.

How to Prevent ASD

My first suggestion is to never place an awake infant in a room with a video device. If the caregivers are watching television and the infant is in the same room, the infant always should be turned away from the screen or covered in such a way that that he does not see the screen, especially any faces. *The only eyes an infant should see move are the ones found in the faces of living beings. Likewise, the sounds of language should come only from the mouths of living people.*

This idea of keeping your infants safe from TV and video exposure is very different than current cultural norms. Like the restaurant owner in the 1950s who forbade smoking, be prepared for comments from the ignorant and uninformed. Remember protecting your infants comes first. Hopefully cultural attitudes will change soon.

If the infant is in a daycare setting, the facility must follow the same rules, no television around or near any baby, infant, or toddler. It is not clear how much television or video exposure it takes to impair a baby's interest in social interaction. Could one exposure at the right time be all it takes? Perhaps, for a certain child. We are so used to watching television we forget what an astonishing experience it was the first time we saw an image of a person talking and moving across a video screen. I am speculating, but I suppose one viewing could be enough to change the way an infant sees the world around him.

The idea to avoid exposure to TV and video devices before the age of two is not a new suggestion. It is the current recommendation from the American Academy of Pediatrics. The Academy for almost the last 15 years has stated no video screens should be present in the child's life until two years of age. They give a variety of reasons for this recommendation, and I will add the prevention of ASD to that list. After all, why take a chance with your baby?

During the first few months of life, while an infant lacks much ability to communicate back, most mothers find their baby's every movement and expression a thing of beauty and wonder. As a parent, I suggest, you give into these feelings and spend as much time as you can playing with your baby. Talk, dress, undress, dress again, kiss, feed, clean and then talk to your baby some more.

Turn off the television, computer and cell phone when you are with your baby. No multitasking allowed. Take an extended leave of absence from work if you can. And please, talk to your friends and family members who are having babies; be a positive part of their social lives as well. Encourage them to also avoid The Pied Pipers of Autism. Visit the new mother and admire the baby. Hold the baby, talk in your best Motherese voice, and give the baby lots of kisses. Act as if you are jealous of the new mother with her beautiful baby.

In our social networks, as in our culture, we need to uphold the idea that maternity and childcare are important and valuable. We need to see mothers and other caregivers glorified and truly supported. After all it takes more than feeding and cleaning a baby to establish a truly empathetic relationship. Remember, some babies especially boys, are not easily wooed into world of two-way communication.

I personally think making a mother return to work six weeks after having a baby is a sad reflection of the current values in our culture. It may be good for business but it is bad for the nation. This reflects a poor understanding of the value of having children truly prepared to assume their roles in our country's social networks.

My second suggestion is no talking toys. The most interesting thing in an infant's environment should be you, the caregiver. In particular it should be your words, your face, your movements and your touch. If a toy delights or captures your baby's attention more than your presence does, then get rid of that toy. Brightly colored toys will capture the infant's attention, but they will never teach social interaction.

Talking toys are positively confusing to infants. Only allow your baby to hear speech when it is being done by people and, best of all, face-to-face, where he can see the lips move. This is one of those situations where the most expensive electronic toys money can buy are the worst things for the baby. If you must buy something fancy and expensive for a baby, buy clothes or something else that encourages caregiver- baby interactions.

My third suggestion is as the infant becomes a toddler, to have socially interactive creatures in your toddler's environment. Neurotypical siblings and dogs are best. The breed of dog should be child-friendly, of course. The dog will give your toddler a lot of attention and communicate in a way that just delights him.

A sibling or a cousin will likely be a key person in your toddler's social network for life. He or she will communicate with the toddler in a way more developmentally closer to your toddler's than you. I remember as a child how I often could express my thoughts to my older brother better than to my mother. I would be amazed as he would then translate my thoughts into language my mother could understand. I learned a lot about social communication and language this way.

However an older sibling with ASD will be a very poor model for a newborn infant. Naturally, the infant's attention will be drawn to their older sibling. But communication with an older sibling with ASD is, sadly enough, going to be one-way. There is not going to be the back and forth eye contact and conversation found in two-way reciprocal social interactions. The older child with ASD, more or less in his own world, is not going to be in the position to offer the younger sibling any real affection or social attention.

There has been a recent study showing a 20% risk of ASD to the child born into a family where one child already has ASD. This is an astonishingly high risk. I think the older child with ASD can be a source and model of one-way communication. This is a situation demanding special vigilance from the usual Pied Pipers of Autism. But that will not be enough since the older sibling with ASD will be another big source of one-way communication.

I do not think there can be any dogmatic solution to this problem; every family is going to be different. I say this since I think a sociable newborn might be just the thing to help the older sibling break out of his social isolation. The experiments I talked about in Chapter 6 showed the only thing that helped a monkey raised in social isolation to become sociable again was the company of a normal younger monkey. Perhaps the situation in human families is similar.

If it is, then contact between a sociable newborn might help the older child with ASD. I think as a parent you will have to watch the behavior of both children very carefully.

If the child with ASD is not making any social connection at all to the newborn then the risk to baby in this relationship is not worth the possible benefit to the child with ASD.

If the infant starts imitating his older brother's un-social behavior then the contact between the two must be limited. By this I mean failing to show good eye contact or interest in joint attention experiences at the proper age. The dicey part is during the first year of the life, the signs of disturbed social communication are going to be subtle.

I also have some other suggestions pertaining to special situations.

Identical Twins

Starting from inside the uterus identical twins can form such a strong twin-twin connection that it can separate them from the rest of their social world. Together they can form a kind of autism-of-two with each twin becoming a strong source of one-way communication for the other.

To prevent this, they should have separate cribs and be treated as separate human beings. For instance, they should be marked with their own names, so everyone who comes in contact with them knows exactly what to call each of them. The people they come in contact with should be encouraged to think of them as separate infants, not just 'The Twins".

Fraternal Twins

Fraternal twins are less prone to ASD, but still the prudent parent should take care to establish separate lines of communication with each baby. Twin-twin communication, although totally cute and charming, needs to be limited so that each twin will be given the opportunity to form his own strong bond to each of the other family members.

Blind Newborns

Loss of vision can be an obstacle to the development of two-way communication. A child born without vision needs a way to establish 'eye contact' with its caregiver; a way of capturing attention and sharing experiences with the people around them. Using talk and touch, a caregiver can establish channels of communication that will make up for the loss of the vision. If a child cannot look into your eyes, he can at least readily feel your touch as a way of knowing he has your attention.

The baby should always know where his caregiver is, and since the baby cannot see, touch is the best substitute. Perhaps a papoose would work well.

As the infant grows, you as the caregiver should use all the other senses, including hearing and smelling, to create and share in joint attention experiences with the child. Have the blind infant explore the world *with you*. I believe this should facilitate normal social development in these children.

Deaf Newborns

A child born with impaired hearing should have someone in their life, from six months on or earlier, who can sign with them. Ideally, it should be a family member.

The preventative measures I am proposing are certainly harmless. No one has ever shown that television exposure or infant videos provide one iota of benefit to babies or toddlers. This risk of giving your child autism is too great. Right now the chances your baby boy will develop ASD are one in seventy.

The Amish do not surround their babies with these electronic video devices. The incidence of ASD in this community is much less than the rest of the country. There is something to be learned from their experience. The changes I propose bring back infant rearing more to the way it has been practiced for thousands of years before the invasion of the Pied Pipers of Autism.

I have not talked much in this book about the difficulties of caring for a child with ASD and how it breaks up and impoverishes families. That deserves another entire book. I am just saying that even if the chances of preventing ASD by the measures I am proposing are only partially effective, it would be well worth the trouble of ridding the Pied Pipers of Autism from your baby's surroundings.

Genetics aside, if the Pied Pipers of Autism are the main environmental cause for ASD, and we banish them from our nurseries, I think more than 90% of the children with ASD that we are seeing today in our families and schools could be prevented.

Research

These suggestions seem to me reasonable, safe and not overwhelmingly difficult. These are steps a prudent parent can take today to insure their infant develops the communication skills they will need to make friends and form social relationships in the life they have in front of them.

But more research needs to be done. The hypothesis discussed in this book is a bit of creative thought and a bit of putting 2 + 2= 4 together. Nevertheless, there are many more experiments and studies in this area needing to be done. Today's ideas are always improved with further study. Meanwhile 'The Integrated Theory of Autism' is, in my opinion, an excellent working hypothesis, one parents need to act on now.

A lot of research on the genetics of autism already has been and continues to be done. All kinds of candidate genes have been found, and hopefully more will be discovered. This new knowledge will help us understand the nature of communication and consciousness in our brains and its connection to our genome. These very important questions touch on the very nature of our existence.

Recently, in 2013, more studies are appearing that look for an environmental factor to explain the cause of ASD. In particular they are looking at chemical exposures during pregnancy. Again advances in the technology of science are paving the way for these new studies. We are now able to detect truly tiny amounts of hundreds of chemicals in the water we drink and the air we breathe. The composition of these chemicals in the air differs from locale to locale depending on the sources of air pollution in any area.

Could a tiny tiny amount of one of these chemicals enter the mother, cross the placenta, enter the baby's blood stream, cross into their brain, and there cause some specific change triggering the subsequent development of ASD in a child? It seems like a stretch to me but the studies are being done. Studies have been reported comparing the incidence of ASD in areas where air pollution is known to be high to other areas without so much of this problem. These studies have shown a linkage between air pollution and ASD.

Is this a surprise? No, these studies confirm what we already learned from Dr.Waldman's study, 'Does Television Cause Autism?" in Chapter 7. Just like rainy weather keeps babies inside, so must air pollution. I would think caregivers would be more concerned about having their babies exposed to polluted air than getting a little wet in the rain. Either way babies would tend to stay inside. And what are babies going to be exposed to inside? The air maybe better but in today's world it is likely they will be surrounded by The Pied Pipers of Autism and one-way communication.

Pollution and genetics may be contributing directly or indirectly to the epidemic of ASD we are living through. Nevertheless we also need to study the development of social communication in infancy with a special focus on those things, such as one-way communication, that can disturb this development. I believe this is the research that will explain the frightening increase of ASD in the world at this time.

The difference between the sexes is another tantalizing area of research. It is almost taboo to suggest that males and females could be inherently different in an area as fundamentally important as social communication, but there it is, evident in the vastly different rates of ASD between boys and girls.

As the reader knows, I am physician, a family physician. This has given me a special perspective on families throughout the 30-plus years I have been in practice in Merced, California. I have delivered hundreds of babies and have been in the wonderful position to watch many of them grow up and have their own families. I have taken care of the baby, the mother, the father, the grandparents, friends of the family, fellow church members, people who came from the same village in Mexico and so on.

I have been able to see my patients not only as individuals but as part of greater social networks. Many times I have seen the individual defer to and sacrifice for the good of the social network they are a part of. Autism is fundamentally a loss of social communication. The child with ASD completely or partially loses connections with the people who form the social networks he could be an important part of.

As such, I think family physicians and pediatricians are in a vital position to develop the research that will answer the question of what is disturbing normal social development and causing the increasing incidence of ASD, and what needs to be done to slow down or stop this problem.

I remember a time, before Sudden Infant Death Syndrome (SIDS) was well understood, when many infants were dying mysteriously. Then someone figured out that something very simple was killing these infants: too many pillows and the wrong sleeping position were the culprits.

It was not the parent's fault; it was just nobody knew how dangerous these practices were. The doctors were advising parents to use the wrong sleeping position and parents were following the fashion of having lots of pillows in the baby's crib. A simple change in the recommendations by the family's primary care providers and a publicity campaign by the public health authorities and the situation improved much to the better.

The improvement happened dramatically and quickly. Someday someone should write a play or a movie about this chain of events. My dream is ASD will someday soon be the same story; the simple changes I am suggesting in this chapter will become widespread and the incidence of the ASD will dramatically fall as well.

The research needing to be done will not be easy but is certainly doable. There could be controlled trials with some groups of infants and toddlers exposed to the normal glut of one-way communication found today in most nurseries and others not.

Another way to do the research, the best way, would be for our culture to make the changes I have proposed, which at the very least are simple and harmless, and watch the incidence statistics show fewer and fewer new children being diagnosed with ASD each year. This is what happened in the case of the Sudden Infant Death Syndrome. Who knows, perhaps the social communication skills and the social relationships for a whole new generation might improve at the same time.

About Otto- Rosangela's Story
Conclusion

Having a kid with Asperger's gives us a lot of work; he needs a lot of our care, attention and too much of our patience, but I guess every child needs some of those things too.

Even though it may seem terrible to have a special needs child, children with Asperger's are special in a good way too. Otto is intelligent, funny, he's got a good heart, he is never mean to anyone, he isn't selfish, he is naïve; sometimes other children takes advantage of his naivety and take toys or other things from him. If they need to take turns to play a videogame for example, Otto doesn't require his turn and the other kids easily mislead him.

Truth is really important for him. If I need to go out and leave him in someone's house, he wants me to tell him that I leaving and say goodbye, even though he would be sad to stay there without me. He also doesn't like to say "black people," he rather says "brown people".

At home he rarely fights with his brother, they both share toys, food, candies, clothes, they get along amazingly. I love my boys and I am very proud of them!

- Rosangela Eichler

Conclusion
Opposition & Reactions

Reactions from the Media Companies

As I complete this book, I am starting to think about what might happen after the book is published. If it is not ignored, I imagine I am going to run into some determined opposition to my theory. I feel a little like David taking on Goliath. The business of making toys and "edutainment" for infants is a big business with many very influential and powerful corporations profiting from these sales.

I cannot help wondering whether I will be attacked personally. I cannot imagine these corporations will not fight against this idea. They will take a page from the same techniques the tobacco companies have used for years. They will say more research needs to be done before any changes are made in how infants are raised in our culture.

They will say something like- 'Dr. Oestreicher's book raises more questions than answers', something to lull the general public into complacency. Then they will sponsor research that is misleading and confusing to delay implementation of these needed changes in the lives of our infants.

Disney nearly sued the University of Washington when they published a study documenting *Baby Einstein* videos did not help infants learn anything, let alone become baby Einsteins. I think this well-known episode has had a chilling effect on any further research in this area. No one wants to be sued by Disney.

Reactions from the Genetic Research Community

Another area of opposition will come from the genetics research industry. I personally admire the great strides made in the understanding of genetics during my lifetime. I believe soon we will all be getting a copy of our baby's genome shortly after birth.

The genetic understanding of ASD would have been a huge triumph for genetic medicine. Unfortunately, the twin studies until recently have led us down the wrong path, ignoring the search for a potentially important environmental factor. When it comes to the importance of genetic causes of ASD, sometimes I feel like I am watching one of those old Westerns where the posse is headed in the wrong direction. We need to turn that posse around and catch the environmental factor or factors causing this pandemic.

I imagine this book will be receiving a lot of criticism from academic and entrepreneurial geneticists. I am sure there is much to learn of great value about all the different genes that increase susceptibility to ASD. I just do not want to see confusion about genetics delaying the implementation of the changes we need to make in the nursery. Infants and toddlers need to get away from video devices and the Pied Pipers of Autism. Genetics are important, but not nearly the whole story.

I am sure I am not prepared for all this opposition. After all, I am just a quiet family physician in a small town in America who has no interest in battling anyone. I would like to just keep taking care of my family and my patients.

By writing this book, I am hoping to do my part to prevent all the future Ottos in the world from developing ASD. Every time I see a child with ASD, I think this did not have to happen and I wonder what this child would have been like if they had not been exposed to the Pied Pipers of Autism in infancy. I get frustrated and angry.

Reactions from Those Parents with Children with ASD

As I have started to circulate this book to families with children who have ASD, I have become aware the book touches a nerve. At times, a family member will remember the first time their child with ASD saw a video or started watching television. They remember how a previously difficult baby suddenly settled down and focused on the video screen.

Of course, the family felt very comfortable with this, since the marketing portrayed such positive things for this form of *edu-tainment*. Not only was the video pleasing and entertaining to their infants but they believed they were helping their baby's intellectual development— Making little Einsteins or Mozarts out of an otherwise difficult baby.

Thanks to this marketing, this kind of activity for the baby was supported by the family's social network and the culture as a whole. And now this book is saying these innocent videos, TV shows and toys are the cause of their child's ASD and all the suffering this has brought. Dr. Oestreicher is saying if we had avoided these kinds of exposures during the first year of life of our child he would not have ASD. How could that be true? Dr. Oestreicher must be a little mad.

First, let me be clear, that is exactly what I am saying and that is the message of this book. Please, do not kill the messenger. I, too, only want to see the end of this outbreak of ASD now. I hold those people who marketed these products to infants without adequately studying the repercussions fully responsible for this debacle and all the suffering it has caused to countless children and families around the world. Why would anyone choose to market these products to infants and change the course of this pivotal vital time of childhood, without knowing what the consequences might eventually be?

The makers of infant formulas at least test to see that babies grow normally with their formulas. When you make extravagant claims that you have a product that is going to benefit all babies and turn them into little Einsteins without a shred of evidence to that effect and the product ends up doing devastating harm to millions of children, I think that is reckless gambling with the future of our children for a paltry profit. If this kind of activity is not criminal, it should be.

When I think of the difficulties that Rosangela and her family go through with Otto, the great bravery so many families show in face of these at times overwhelming problems, and when I think it could have all been avoided by simple measures, it does drive me mad with anger.

So getting back to families with children with autism, their first reaction to the book is often denial. They think there must be something else causing ASD, something the book is missing. After all millions of dollars are being spent each year trying to understand ASD, how can something so simple have been missed? All I have to say to this point is I am not the first person to make this connection. The American Academy of Pediatrics, to their credit, has opposed video devices during infancy for years now.

Twin studies, quite inadvertently, seriously set back research in autism for years. I think when a research finding hits the cultural mind set just right, it can set off an explosion of activity, in this case trying to prove the genetic origins of ASD.

This book is born out of all the research done in the last 20 years. 98% of what I say in this book comes directly out of this research. I think the vaccine story misled many people as well but at least they were right in looking for a cause in the environment of the infant, something the academics were missing.

Maybe the mass media is so pervasive now that most investigators do not even see the incredible effect it has on modern life even in infancy. Just the same, whatever happened before, the effect of one-way communication on infants was missed until now.

After denial, some parents and families are going to feel guilt and remorse. Why didn't I notice how attached my child was getting to TV and videos and how distant he was getting from me? Why didn't I make the connection and change things? They are going to think of a million things they might have done otherwise that might have made a difference.

I find it impossible to express my feelings to such parents on paper. The one-way communication writing a book provides just does not do.

I would like to meet such parents in person and listen to your story from the beginning, hear about your hopes, your disappointments, what happened, how you tried to make sense of it all, how you struggled, and how you still loved your child despite all the difficulties. Since we would be face-to-face, you would know that I was really listening, listening with my heart, and felt your pain.

I would say something like this to you: you seem like a good decent person and a caring loving parent but that somehow in the last 50 years things have gotten twisted in our culture for infants. I would also add that there was nothing you did that millions of other parents are not doing even now.

You would know my words were sincere and heartfelt since you could hear and see me talk, feel my presence and our eyes would meet. At the end of the meeting, nothing would have changed, nothing would have been solved. But we both would have shared the consolation we all need in the face of the bitterness that is too often a part of life. The consolation would have come through human contact, human contact by means of two-way face-to-face communication, the best communication we have.

Reactions from Parents- In General

I also expect some opposition from parents in general. After all, I kind of feel like the Grinch who stole Christmas with my opposition to toys for infants and toddlers. What could be wrong with toys kids enjoy?

I think the situation is like diabetes in children today: the children need food to grow but as parents, we need to help our children get a grip on overeating. Too many tasty and rich foods are extensively marketed and are easily available in the culture in which we live. They come disguised as being 'nutritious' when they are really just tuned to children's tastes and in a sense addictive. It is the kind of food some children just cannot get enough of. Too much tasty food and our children become first fat and then diabetic.

It starts with well-meaning parents and too many easy tasty choices. Toys are the same; they come disguised as 'educational,' when they really just distract infants from the social interactions that are the most important part of the first year of life. Infants and toddlers do not need to be 'educated' to become little Einsteins or Mozarts. They need to learn to become an important part of a mutually trusting social network, their family.

Television in such a short time has become so prevalent everywhere. It is almost part of the scenery, the background of our lives. As adults who have lived with television all our lives, it is hard to imagine how something as basic as television could affect infants and toddlers so much and cause ASD.

Part of the problem is we have long forgotten what astonishing things the video screen and television are. To see a moving, talking image of a living human being in front of us for the first time is startling. It is something our infants have not been prepared by evolution to make sense of. They have evolved to use these same cues to find friendship, attention and love from living people in their family.

I also think the problem is as adults we cannot remember what a profound effect a developmental stage properly unfolding can have on us. This is especially true for infants because they are just starting out in life and their brains are changing so rapidly. And then none of us have any memory for that period of time in our own life.

To better understand this phenomenon, I like to compare it to puberty a period of time we can still recall from own lives. I remember passing through puberty and being puzzled and amazed about how differently I felt about girls from one year to the next. All of a sudden, my mind and brain were changing, and my interests and my cravings were all turned around and fired up.

To understand infancy, I imagine, is to understand infants have similar cravings; only in this case it is for language acquisition and social communication. They look to their environment for words, faces, movements, etc.; all means of communication. For hundreds of thousands of years, these cravings led infants directly into social interactions with the people who loved and cared for them.

Talking toys, video devices and television are the Pied Pipers of Autism. They have caused a massive exposure to one-way communication in the today's nursery. This exposure satisfies the infant's intense craving to understand and to bind to the world around them, but unfortunately, they are social dead ends. In genetically susceptible infants they ultimately lead to social isolation and ASD. This is The Integrated Theory of Autism.

Leonard Oestreicher, MD

Merced, California

May 1, 2012

Friend Us at Facebook – Pied Pipers of Autism

Email the Author at "l.oestreicher@toystvautism.com"

About the Author

I was born in 1948 in Newark, New Jersey. My family moved to the suburbs of New York City before my second birthday. We moved to Levittown and I vaguely remember the excitement of having a TV already built into the living room of our tiny house. My brother, Donald, and I spent many hours as kids watching that set. I remember that my father disapproved of television, an attitude which I thought at the time was hopelessly provincial and old fashioned.

My father was an attorney who worked for Sperry Rand. He died of a heart attack at home. I was only eight years old. My idea to become a physician, I think, stems from the grief I felt with his death. Although I can hardly remember him, his picture is always by my desk. It gives me some kind of comfort.

My mother, then a widower, quickly finished college and became a teacher, a field open to women at the time. My brother and I became latchkey children, given a lot of leeway and responsibility. We freely roamed the streets of Great Neck, NY, returning home for meals and chores. Mom expected dinner on the table when she returned from work, so I learned to cook meals for the family at a young age.

Great Neck, at that time in the early 1960's, was an upper middle class, largely Jewish, enclave full of bright and politically active teen agers. I was a mediocre student. My mother considered me an underachiever and had the school test my IQ. After I was tested the school agreed. I understood this was a big thing for my mother, but it did not change my academic ways. Later on, when I got an 800 on my math SAT's, I got the attention of the whole high school for a day but I continued to be a lackadaisical student.

I was very active in the Civil Rights movement in high school. Marijuana and the whole counterculture thing was just finding its way into the suburbs. My friends and I made many pilgrimages to Greenwich Village to observe and emulate the 'beatnik' generation.

After graduating from high school, I went to college at the University of Wisconsin at Madison. I had burnt out on political activism and decided to actually focus on my schoolwork to see if I could qualify to get into medical school. My grades, to my astonishment, actually got quite good and soon enough I was applying to medical school. My dream was to go to medical school at UCSF and after a long wait, my dream came true. I was thrilled to be in medical school and in San Francisco, the most beautiful and interesting city that I have found in the world.

I always wanted to be a family practitioner, on the front lines of helping people, getting to know families for the long run. In this way my career prepared me for this very book. My experiences getting to know people over time in the context of their families and communities has given me the perspective to understand the importance and the workings of social networks. The links of trust, that tie all social networks together and take us to our collective futures and that are so important for all of us, are the daily work of the family practitioner.

The focus on prevention of health problems is another important part of our work as family practitioners. In the end *The Pied Pipers of Autism*'s most important message is a message of prevention and is aimed at all the future children who are at risk for this disheartening disorder.

As family practitioners, we have to synthesize the findings from the many medical specialties to form a coherent practice for the benefit of our patients. This involves integrating studies drawn from many different fields, weighing the important gems from the overhyped pronouncements. This was another skill which proved essential in the formation of this book.

So, in a very real way, the choice of Family Practice prepared me for *The Pied Pipers of Autism*. The other aspect of my life that prepared me to be the author of this book was my family life. I married shortly after my training was complete and had a family with my first wife, Caroline. Daniel, Emily, and Alex were born five years apart starting in 1975. They have all become fine people and I am very proud to be their father.

And then in 2009, I became a father once again with Roseli, my current wife. So I have had a special opportunity to observe and be a part of three generations. The first was my own childhood, in the 50's, the second, my first family, in the 70's and 80's, and now again with Giovanna. In between, I have been involved with lives of my patients and their families.

As a result I have an unusually broad personal experience on the nature and norms of childrearing during this period of time and how they have changed. During this same time period ASD has emerged from being a very rare to a common disorder. My experience comes not just from reading books or looking at hundreds of studies, but from being there, not just being an observer but a participant in the beautiful process of development in infants and children.

So in short, while I have not spent my life in academia studying autism, I feel my life has prepared me to be the author of this book.

- Leonard Oestreicher, MD

Glossary

A

APPLIED BEHAVIOR ANALYSIS (ABA)
Applied Behavior Analysis is the design, implementation and evaluation of environmental modifications to produce socially significant improvement in human behavior. ABA includes the use of direct observation, measurement and functional analysis of the relations between environment and behavior. Thus, it focuses on explaining behavior in terms of external events that can be manipulated rather than internal constructs that are beyond our understanding. The principles come from operant conditioning, which is simply shaping behavior with rewards and punishments.

AREA 17 / AREA 18
Two specific Bordman area locations in the visual cortex. They were first described by scientist Korbinian Brodmann in his early analyses of neuro-anatomy.

ASPERGER'S SYNDROME (ASPERGER'S SYNDROME)
A developmental disorder related to autism and characterized by the preservation of cognitive and language abilities with impaired social skills and restrictive, repetitive patterns of interest and activities. However, they are generally on the high functioning end of the spectrum.

ATTENTION
As attention is the key precursor to learning, the brain is in a state ready to learn and react to a stimulus. The elements of attention are alertness, a need-based state and a goal that hopefully can be realized.

AUTISTIC-LIKE

Some disorders or syndromes result in humans (and in some cases social animals such as non-human primates) exhibiting symptoms similar to ASD.
AXON
The long thread like part of a neuron along which impulses are conducted away from the cell body of the neuron, or soma, and towards other cells.

B

[TO] BABBLE / BABBLING (IN INFANTS)
Babbling is a crucial component of child development as well as early language acquisition. During this time an infant appears to be experimenting with uttering the sounds or phonemes of their native language, or mother tongue, but not yet producing any recognizable words.
BABY EINSTEIN
Baby Einstein is a line of multimedia products and toys that specializes in activities for children aged 3 months to 3 years old.
BABY TALK
See MOTHERESE.
BACKGROUND TELEVISION
The changes in color, sound, shapes and motion as part of the programming of television that attract attention. Background television is the non-content part of television programming.
BEHAVIOR
Behavior is the observable manifestations of brain activity. Our brain, the central nervous system, controls the actions of our body, via the peripheral nervous system, which in turn produces these observable behaviors, actions and mannerisms.
BLANK STARING
This is an occasional symptom whereby the act of staring is not accompanied by the usual emotional facial expressions rather showing detachment particularly in regards to social interactions.
BLIND (BLINDED EXPERIMENT)
A blind or blinded experiment is a scientific experiment where some of the people involved are prevented from knowing certain

information that might lead to conscious or subconscious bias on their part, invalidating the results.

BRAIN ACTIVITY
As an area in the brain becomes metabolically active, the blood flow to that area increases. This can be seen on the fMRI and demonstrate which areas of the brain are involved in a certain behavior, the neural network for that behavior.

BROCA'S AREA
Broca's area is a region of the human brain with functions linked to language ability in general and speech production (also referred to as expressive language) more specifically. It is located in the frontal lobe at the inferior frontal gyrus.

C

CAREGIVER
An individual, such as a parent, foster parent, or head of a household, who attends to the needs of a child or dependent adult. Caregiver for infants and young children is usually the mother.

CEREBELLUM
The cerebellum (Latin for little brain) is a region of the brain that plays an important role in motor control and sensory coordination.

CHROMOSOME
A chromosome is an organized structure of DNA and protein found in cells. It is a single piece of coiled DNA containing many genes, regulatory elements and other nucleotide sequences. Chromosomes also contain DNA-bound proteins, which serve to package the DNA and control its functions.

COGNITION
Cognition refers to mental processes. These processes include attention, remembering, producing and understanding language, solving problems, and making decisions.

COMMUNICATION
Communication can be verbal, such as spoken language, or non-verbal, such as facial expressions or gestures. Successful communication depends on the receiver having a prior acquired set of expectations and mutually understood channel of communication

where the signals of communication pass from the sender to the receiver.
COMMUNICATION, CHANNELS OF
The means by which communication signals such as language pass from the sender to the receiver.
COMPUTERESE
The synthetic voice of talking toys that mimics the human voice.
CONCORDANCE
(In genetic studies) The degree of similarity in a pair of twins with respect to the presence or absence of a particular disease or trait.
CONSTELLATION OF BEHAVIORS
A related group of behaviors usually found together.
CONTROL GROUP
The practice of assigning parameters of some phenomenon to be observed or studied not occurring in one group (negative), but occurring in the other group (positive). These control groups then serve the purpose of limiting confounding variables which can alter results and cause conclusions to be reached that are not in concordance with the scientific method.
CONTROLLED TRIAL
A randomized controlled trial (RCT) is a type of scientific experiment. The key distinguishing feature of the usual RCT is that study subjects, after assessment of eligibility and recruitment, but before the intervention to be studied begins, are randomly assigned to the either the control or the experimental arm.
CORE DEFECT
The defining or primary symptom of some disorder or disease.
CORTEX, CEREBRAL
The cerebral cortex is a sheet of neural tissue that is outermost to the cerebrum of the mammalian brain. It plays a key role in memory, attention, perceptual awareness, thought, language, and consciousness.
CORTEX, VISUAL
The visual cortex of the brain is the part of the cerebral cortex responsible for processing visual information. It is located in the occipital lobe, in the back of the brain.
COURTSHIP

The pattern of behaviors and interactions that precede the mating of two individuals of a species.

CRITICAL PERIOD
In general, a critical period is a limited time in which an event can occur, usually to result in some kind of transformation. A "critical period" in developmental psychology and developmental biology is a time in the early stages of an organism's life during which it displays a heightened sensitivity to certain environmental stimuli, and develops in particular ways due to experiences at this time. If the organism does not receive the appropriate stimulus during this "critical period", it may be difficult, ultimately less successful, or even impossible, to develop some functions later in life.

D

DENDRITE
Dendrites are the branched projections of a neuron that act to conduct the electrochemical stimulation received from other neural cells to the cell body, or soma, of the neuron from which the dendrites project.

DEPTH PERCEPTION
Depth perception is the visual ability to perceive the world in three dimensions (3D) and the distance of an object.

DIZYGOTIC TWINS (DZ)
Twin siblings that grew from two different ovum. As such, they have a different genetic makeup.

DNA (GENETIC MATERIAL)
Deoxyribonucleic acid is a nucleic acid that contains the genetic instructions used in the development and functioning of all known living organisms (with the exception of RNA viruses). The DNA segments that carry this genetic information are called genes.

E

EDU-TAINMENT
Varying products that are marketed to parents as being both entertaining and educational for their children.

ELECTRO-BIOCHEMICAL REACTION
A term coined by author referring the biochemical reactions and the electrical impulses that are generated by biochemical reactions that take place in the nervous system.
EMPATHY
Empathy is the capacity to recognize and, to some extent, share feelings (such as sadness or happiness) that are being experienced by another being.
ESTROGEN
Estrogens are the primary female sex hormones.
EXPRESSIVE VOCAL COMMUNICATION
The act of communicating vocally by using our larynges to speak, sing, shout or scream.
EXTREME MALE BRAIN THEORY OF AUTISM
A theory proposed that there are basically that there are two types of brains: male and female. The differences in the brains are caused by the second surge of testosterone in the male. This surge, according to Baron-Cohen, makes the male brain more systemizing and less empathetic compared to the female brain.
EXECUTIVE FUNCTION
These functions are largely carried out by prefrontal areas of the frontal lobe. Executive function is an umbrella term for cognitive processes such as planning, working memory, attention, problem solving, verbal reasoning, inhibition, mental flexibility, multi-tasking, initiation and monitoring of actions.
EYE CONTACT
Eye contact is a meeting of the eyes between two individuals. In human beings, eye contact is a form of nonverbal communication and is thought to have a large influence on social behavior.
EYE GAZING
The act of looking with intent.

F

FACILITY in SOCIAL COMMUNICATION
The ability to understand, process, and respond to social cues without undue effort almost intuitively. It corresponds to fluency in language usage.

FERAL CHILD
A feral child (also, colloquially, wild child) is a human child who has lived isolated from human contact from a very young age, and has no (or little) experience of human care, loving or social behavior, and, crucially, of human language.

FLAPPING
A behavior that is similar to rocking but involves arm movements.

FLUENCY
The highest level of proficiency in language acquisition.

FLUOROSCEIN DYES
Fluorescent dyes that are used in various medical imaging procedures to create a greater contrast so that observers may analyze the physiologic activity with greater accuracy.

fMRI SCAN (FUNCTIONAL MAGNETIC RESONANCE IMAGING)
a type of specialized MRI scan used to measure the hemodynamic response (change in blood flow) related to neural activity in the brain or spinal cord of humans or other animals.

FMR1 (GENE: FRAGILE X MENTAL RETARDATION 1)
FMR1 (fragile X mental retardation 1) is a human gene that codes for a protein called fragile X mental retardation protein, or FMRP. This protein, most commonly found in the brain, is essential for normal cognitive development and female reproductive function. Mutations of this gene can lead to Fragile X syndrome, mental retardation, premature ovarian failure, autism, Parkinson's disease, developmental delays and other features that are found in ASD.

FOXP2 (GENE)
Forkhead box protein P2 also known as FOXP2 is a protein that in humans is encoded by the FOXP2 gene, located on human chromosome 7 In humans, mutations of FOXP2 cause a severe speech and language disorder. Versions of FOXP2 exist in similar forms in distantly related vertebrates; functional studies of the gene in mice and in songbirds indicate that it is important for modulating plasticity of neural circuits.

FRAGILE X SYNDROME
Fragile X syndrome is a genetic syndrome that is the most commonly known single-gene cause of autism and intellectual disability

FRATERNAL TWINS

See DIZYGOTIC TWINS (DZ).
FRONTAL LOBE
The frontal lobe is an area in the brain of humans and other mammals, located at the front of each cerebral hemisphere. The precentral gyrus, forming the posterior border of the frontal lobe, contains the primary motor cortex, which controls voluntary movements of specific body parts.

G

GAIT
Gait is the act and manner of walking.
GENDER
Gender is a range of characteristics used to distinguish between males and females, particularly in the cases of men and women and the masculine and feminine attributes assigned to them.
GENE
A gene is a unit of heredity of a living organism. It is a name given to some stretches of DNA and RNA that code for a polypeptide or for an RNA chain that has a function in the organism. Living beings depend on genes, as they specify all proteins and functional RNA chains. Genes hold the information to build and maintain an organism's cells and pass genetic traits to offspring.
GENETIC LINKAGE
Genetic linkage is the tendency of certain loci or alleles to be inherited together. Genetic loci that are physically close to one another on the same chromosome tend to stay together during meiosis, and are thus genetically linked.
GENETIC MUTATION
The random nature of genetic mutation, which happens very often during transcription of DNA and RNA, is one of the most fundamental causes of genetic diversity in the overall population of a species
GENETIC PREDISPOSITION
Due to the powerful influences of genetics, some people are genetically predisposed, that is to say innately more likely, to develop certain skills or behavioral traits.
GENOME

The complete set of genetic information for a living being.
GENOTYPE
The genotype of an organism is the inherited instructions it carries within its genome.
GESTURING
A form of non-verbal (or pre-verbal) communication by which either the child or caregiver uses physical movement to communicate emotions and initiate or continue episodes of joint attention.
GLIA
Glial cells, sometimes called neuroglia or simply glia, are non-neuronal cells that maintain homeostasis, form myelin, and provide support and protection for neurons in the brain.

H

HEBBIAN LEARNING
Hebbian theory describes a basic mechanism for synaptic plasticity wherein an increase in synaptic efficacy arises from the presynaptic cell's repeated and persistent stimulation of the postsynaptic cell. Introduced by Donald Hebb in 1949, it is also called Hebb's rule, Hebb's postulate, and cell assembly theory. The theory is often summarized as "Cells that fire together, wire together."

I

ICE BOX MOTHER
A term used in the early stages of autism research, when it was thought that the condition was caused by emotionally distant or unavailable mothers. In other words, it was thought to be caused by a problem in the maternal-child relationship, an environmental factor.
IDENTITICAL TWINS MONOZYGOTIC TWINS.
IMAGINARY PLAY
A common behavior in neurotypic children involving play that occurs in the realm of imagination. Children suffering from ASD have tremendous difficulty engaging in imaginary social play.
INCIDENCE (EPIDEMIOLOGY)

Incidence is a measure of the risk of developing some new condition within a specified period of time. Thus, incidence conveys information about the risk of contracting the disease, whereas prevalence indicates how widespread the disease is.

INDO-EUROPEAN LANGUAGES
The Indo-European languages are a family (or phylum) of several hundred related languages and dialects, including most major current languages of Europe, the Iranian plateau, and South Asia.

INFLECTION
Alteration in pitch or tone of the voice to convey that the sentence is interrogative or to emphasize a certain part of the utterance.

INHERENT ABILITY
An ability that one is genetically predisposed to have, requiring less effort and time to master than other people.

INITIATED JOINT ATTENTION
An episode of joint attention, the child starts by attracting the attention of his caretaker by using for instance pointing.

INTEGRATED THEORY OF AUTISM
A theory posited in this book that infants who are genetically predisposed to developing ASD can have their precondition exacerbated by of exposure to one-way communication most commonly in the form of television, videos, and toys. This form of communication displaces the fundamentally important face-to-face, two-way communication that allows humans to socially integrate. This failure to socially integrate in the first years of life leads to all the subsequent findings in ASD.

INTELLIGENCE QUOTIENT (IQ)
A quantitative measure of human intelligence.

[TO] INTERPOSITION / INTERPOSITIONING
One of major cues that allows our visual cortex to see stereoscopically where the stimulus that is closer blocks out part of the more distant stimulus.

IRIS
A thin, circular structure in the eye, responsible for controlling the diameter and size of the pupils and thus the amount of light reaching the retina. The colored part of the eye.

IDIOSYNCRATIC REACTION
A reaction to some stimulus that is independent of cultural norms.

J

JOINT ATTENTION
Joint attention is the sharing of a visual experience by the caregiver and the infant. By alternating eye contact between each other and visual experience, both parties learn about each other's reaction to the common experience. Eye contact and joint attention are the fundamental building blocks for all subsequent social communication. Other channels of communication can substitute for vision in joint attention.

K

KINSHIP GROUP
The most fundamental and primal social network in human development as the network is composed of the family. The kinship group includes the family and other 'blood relatives' such as grandparents, cousins, nieces, grandchildren etc. and their families.

L

LARYNX (LARYNGES)
The larynx (plural larynges), commonly called the voice box, is an organ in the neck of amphibians, reptiles and mammals (including humans) involved in breathing, sound production, and protecting the trachea against food aspiration. It manipulates pitch and volume. The larynx houses the vocal folds which are essential for producing the sounds that make up spoken language.
[TO] LEARN
The brain is shaped by interaction with surrounding world. In a broad sense this is called *learning*.
LOW FUNCTIONING AUTISM
A person suffering from ASD that is on the more severe end of the spectrum, thereby very seriously limiting their socialization.

M

MECP2 (GENE)
MECP2 (methyl CpG binding protein 2) is a gene that provides instructions for making its protein product, MECP2, also referred to as MeCP2. MECP2 appears to be essential for the normal function of nerve cells. MECP2 gene mutations are the cause of most cases of Rett syndrome, a progressive neurologic developmental disorder and one of the most common causes of mental retardation in females.

MEMORY
An organism's ability to store, retain, and recall information and experiences.

MENTAL IMITATION
The act of imitating another person's behavior or actions mentally without any accompanying behavior

METABOLISM
Metabolism is the set of chemical reactions that happen in the cells of living organisms to sustain life.

[TO] MIMIC
To copy the behavior of speech on other people.

MIRROR NEURON SYSTEM
There is a special system in the brain, called the *mirror neuron system,* which involves observing the world and then playing back whatever action was observed through the appropriate part of our brain without any actual movement taking place. This system also mirrors sensations and emotions.

MONOZYGOTIC TWINS (MZ)
Twin siblings that grew from a single ovum. As such, they have identical genetic makeup.

MOTHERESE
Motherese is a nonstandard form of speech used by adults in talking to toddlers and infants.
It is usually delivered with a "cooing" pattern of intonation different from that of normal adult speech. Motherese is also characterized by the shortening and simplifying of words.

MRI SCAN (MAGNETIC RESONANCE IMAGING)

A medical imaging technique used in radiology to visualize detailed internal structures. MRI makes use of the property of nuclear magnetic resonance (NMR) to image nuclei of atoms inside the body.
MUTISM
Mutism is the inability to talk.
MYELIN SHEATH
Myelin is a electrically insulating material that forms a layer, the myelin sheath, usually around the axon of a neuron. Myelin accelerates the speeds the conduction of nerve. Once an axon has a myelin sheath the position of the axon is more or less fixed.

N

NEED-BASED STATE
A state of being in which a person is motivated to perform an action or behave to satisfy some need such as hunger, exploration, nurturing, lust etc.
NEURAL NETWORK
For any brain function or behavior there is a neural network, which is a shorthand way of saying a group of anatomic parts of the brain that are involved sequentially in the execution of that function.
NEURON
A neuron is an electrically excitable cell that processes and transmits information by electrical and chemical signaling.
NEURONAL PRUNING
In neuroscience, synaptic pruning, neuronal pruning or axon pruning refer to neurological regulatory processes, which facilitate a change in neural structure by reducing the overall number of neurons and synapses, leaving more efficient synaptic configurations.
NEUROTRANSMITTER
Neurotransmitters are endogenous chemicals that transmit signals from a neuron to a target cell across a synapse.
NEUROTYPICAL (BEHAVIOR)
Behavior that is not outside the spectrum of ordinary or non-pathological behavior in a majority of the human population.

O

OBJECT BLURRING
One of the major cues that allows our visual cortex to see stereoscopically.
OBSERVABLE BEHAVIORS
Behavior that a observer can detect objectively.
OCCIPITAL LOBE (HUMAN BRAIN)
The occipital lobe is the visual processing center of the mammalian brain containing most of the anatomical region of the visual cortex. The primary visual cortex is Brodmann area 17.
ONE-WAY COMMUNICATION
A form of communication whereby one person passively receives the information transmitted from someone or something else. There is no social interaction possible.
OPERANT CONDITIONING
It is the paradigm of shaping behavior with rewards and punishments.

P

PEAK PROFICIENCY
The level of language acquisition in humans when their ability to speak a language is at the level of a native speaker.
PHENOTYPE
A phenotype is an organism's observable characteristics or traits.
PRELITERATE SOCIETIES
A society that has not yet created writing and communicates orally.
PREVALENCE (EPIDIEMOLOGY)
In epidemiology, the prevalence of a health-related state in a population is defined as the total number of cases in the population, divided by the number of individuals in the population. It is used as an estimate of how common a disease is within a population over a certain period of time.
PRIMATE
A group of genetically related animals that are the closest living genetic relatives to humans.

PRIVATE LANGUAGE (TWINS/SIBLINGS)
A phenomenon attested largely in twins or siblings whereby the siblings will develop an idiosyncratic and rich language that is comprehensible only to them. The development of such private languages can be detrimental to a child's development of social communication and may encourage the development of self-involvement.

PROPRIOCEPTION
Proprioception is the sense of the relative position of neighboring parts of the body and strength of effort being employed in movement.

PUBERTY
Puberty is the process of physical changes by which a child's body matures into an adult body capable of sexual reproduction.

R

REACTION
A bodily response to or activity aroused by a stimulus that can be internal or external.

RECIPROCAL IMITATION
An imitative process in which both parties mimic the other.

RETT SYNDROME
Rett syndrome is a neurodevelopmental disorder of the grey matter of the brain that almost exclusively affects females. The clinical features include small hands and feet and a deceleration of the rate of head growth (including microcephaly in some). Repetitive hand movements, such as wringing and/or repeatedly putting hands into the mouth, are also noted. People with Rett syndrome are prone to gastrointestinal disorders and up to 80% have seizures. They typically have no verbal skills, and about 50% of individuals affected are not ambulatory. Scoliosis, growth failure, and constipation are very common and can be problematic. They often have features of ASD.

[TO] ROCK / ROCKING (STEREOTYPIC ACTION)
A stereotypic action that is frequently seen in the constellation of behaviors that are indicative of ASD; it is postulated that this behavior serves as a form of self-comfort.

S

SALLY-ANNE FALSE BELIEF TEST
A test used in determining a child's capacity to form a theory of mind.
SCAFFOLDING
Scaffolding is the provision of sufficient support to future growth and development.
SCRIPTED SPEECH
Speech patterns and structures that sound unnatural in the context of a conversation or a verbal interaction.
SELF COMMUNICATION
Solitary thoughts that are shared socially.
SELF-INVOLVEMENT
Solitary thoughts and behaviors that do not have a social component.
SELF-INVOLVEMENT CRITERIA
This set of criteria is referring to a constellation of behaviors that are found in ASD reflecting the autonomous nature of this condition. These include focused interests, repetitive action, resistance to change and others. The other set of criteria in ASD focus on the loss of social communication and language.
SELF-SACRIFICE
The act of sacrificing one's own interests for the greater good of one's social network.
SENSORY CUE
A sensory cue is a signal that can be extracted from the sensory input by a perceiver, which indicates the state of some property of the world that the perceiver is interested in perceiving.
SENSORY PERCEPTION
The act of perceiving and processing internal or external stimuli.
SHARED INTERESTS/SHARED FUTURE/SHARED PAST
These are basic and fundamental criteria for a group of two or more people to form a social network.
SOCIAL COMMUNICATION
The behavior associated with communicating and relating to other members within one's social network.
SOCIAL HEALTH
The measure of successful integration of a person in to any of their given social networks.

SOCIAL NETWORK
For the purposes of this book, a social network is a social structure made up of individuals which are connected by a common interest, a shared past and an imagined shared future.
SOCIAL REFERENCING
Social referencing is a form of joint attention, where one person learns how to react to a novel event of object by referring to the reaction of the other more experience person.
SOCIALIZATION
Providing an individual with the skills and habits needed to participate in his or her social networks.
SON-RISING PROGRAM
Son-Rise is a home-based program for children with autism spectrum disorders and other developmental disabilities.
STEREOSCOPIC VISION
The ability to see in three dimensions.
STIMS / STIMMING
Stimming is a repetitive body movement, such as hand flapping, which is hypothesized to stimulate one or more senses. The term is shorthand for self-stimulation. Repetitive movement, or stereotypy, is often referred to as stimming under the hypothesis that it has a function related to sensory input.
STIMULUS
A stimulus is a detectable change in the internal or external environment.
SUB-CAPABILITIES
A set of capabilities that needed to perform a certain capability.
SUBJECT
The person that is being observed.
SUSTAINED ATTENTION
Sustained attention is a period of time of attention and alertness.
SYNAPSE
In the nervous system a synapse is a structure that permits a neuron to pass an electrical or chemical signal to another cell (neural or otherwise).
SYNDROMIC AUTISM
A genetic syndrome of children who have some features of ASD but also have distinctive features that are not a part of ASD.

SYNTAX
In linguistics, syntax is the study of the principles and rules for constructing phrases and sentences in natural languages.
SYSTEMIZE / SYSTEMIZING
The process by which some children are more interested in understanding the behavior of things rather than developing an understanding of how living beings with internal intentions behave.

T

TEMPORAL LOBE
The temporal lobe is a region of the cerebral cortex that is located beneath the Sylvian fissure on both cerebral hemispheres of the mammalian brain. The temporal lobe is involved in auditory perception and is home to the primary auditory cortex. The temporal lobe contains the hippocampus and plays a key role in the formation of long-term memory.
TESTOSTERONE
Testosterone is a steroid hormone from the androgen group. It is the principal male sex hormone.
THEORY OF MIND
Theory of mind is the ability to attribute and identify mental states—beliefs, intents, desires, pretending, knowledge, etc. in other beings.
TRAIT
A trait is a distinct variant of an organism that can be identified by an observer which may be inherited, environmentally determined or be a combination of the two.
TWO-WAY COMMUNICATION
A form of communication in which both parties relay information to one another. Two-way communication is the fundamental form of interaction in a social relationship.

V

VISUAL CLIFFS
A visual cliff is a flat surface that visually appears to suddenly fall off.

W

WERNICKE'S AREA (HUMAN BRAIN)
One of the two parts of the cerebral cortex linked since the late nineteenth century to speech (the other is Broca's area). It is involved in the understanding of written and spoken language.

[TO] WOO (CAREGIVER-CHILD INTERACTION)
A behavior in which the caregiver tries to interest the child's attention, trust, and affection.

X

XX (HUMAN CHROMOSOME)
The chromosomal makeup of a female human.
XY (HUMAN CHROMOSOME)
The chromosomal makeup of a male human.
X CHROMOSOME
The X chromosome is one of the two sex-determining chromosomes in many animal species, including mammals (the other is the Y chromosome) and is common in both males and females.

Y

Y CHROMOSOME
The Y chromosome is one of the two sex-determining chromosomes in most mammals, including humans. In mammals, it contains the gene SRY, which triggers testis development if present.

Bibliography

Abrahams, Brett S. & Daniel H. Geschwind. "Genetics of Autism." Vogel and Motulsky's Human Genetics: Problems and Approaches. Speicher, M.R. et al (eds.) 2010; 699-714.

Anderson, Daniel R. & Tiffany A. Pempek. "Television and Very Young Children." American Behavioral Scientist. 2005. 48: 505-522.

Asperger syndrome: Slow response time and the impact of prompting." Research in Autism Spectrum Disorders. 5 (2011): pp 1129–1137.

Baron-Cohen, Simon. "Testing the extreme male brain (EMB) theory of autism: Let the data speak for themselves." Cognitive Neuropsychiatry. 2003. 10(1), 77-81.

Baron-Cohen, Simon. "The extreme male brain theory of autism." TRENDS in Cognitive Sciences. June 2002. Vol. 6 No. 6. Pp 248-254.

Baron-Cohen, Simon. Autism and Asperger Syndrome. London, Oxford University Press, 2008.

Baron-Cohen, Simon. The Essential Difference: men, women and the extreme male brain. Penguin, Allen Lane / Basic Books, 2003.

Beckett, Celia et al. "Behavior Patterns Associated with Institutional Deprivation: A Study of Children Adopted from Romania." Developmental and Behavioral Pediatrics. Vol. 23, No. 5, October 2002.

Belton, Teresa. "Television and imagination: an investigation of the medium's influence on children's story-making." Media Culture. 2001; 23: 799-820.

Bishop, D.V.M. & S.J. Bishop. "'Twin Language': A Risk Factor for Language Impairment?" Journal of Speech, Language, and Hearing Research. February 1998, Vol. 41, pp 150-160.

Boucher, Jill. "Language development in autism." International Congress Series. 1254 (2003) 247 – 253.

Brown, Ari. ""Media Use by Children Younger Than 2 Years." PEDIATRICS. Volume 128, Number 5, November 2011. (COUNCIL ON COMMUNICATIONS AND MEDIA).

Brown, James M. et al. "The path of visual attention." Acta Psychologica. 121 (2006): pp 199–209.

Charman, Tony et al. "Testing joint attention, imitation, and play as infancy precursors to language and theory of mind." Cognitive Development. 15 (2000) pp 481-498.

Charman, Tony. "Why is joint attention a pivotal skill in autism?" Philosophical of the Royal Society London B. 358, 315-324.

Chonchaiya, Weerasak & Chandhita Pruksananonda. "Comparision of television viewing between children with autism spectrum disorder and controls" Acta Pædiatrica. 2011, 100. Pp 1033-1037.

Chonchaiya, Weerasak & Chandhita Pruksananonda. "Television viewing associates with delayed language development." Acta Pædiatrica. 2008, 97. Pp 997-982.

Christakis, Dimitri A. & Michelle M. Garrison. "Preschool-Aged Children's Television Viewing in Child Care Settings." PEDIATRICS. Vol. 124, No. 6 December 2009. Pp 1627-1632.

Cleveland, Allison & Tricia Striano. "The effects of joint attention on object processing in 4- and 9-month-old infants." Infant Behavior & Development. 30 (2007): pp 499–504.

Courage, Mary L. & Alissa E. Setliff. "When babies watch television: Attention-getting, attention-holding, and the implications for learning from video material." Developmental Review. 30 (2010) 220-238.

Courage, Mary L. & Mark L. Howe. "To watch or not to watch: Infants and toddlers in a brave new electronic world." Developmental Review. 30 (2010) 101-115.

Courage, Mary L. et al. "When the television is always on: The impact of infant-directed video on 6- and 18-month-olds' attention during toy play and on parent-infant interaction." Infant Behavior and Development. 33 (2010) 176-188.

Croen L.A., Grether J.K., & Selvin S. 2002. "Descriptive epidemiology of autism in a California population: Who is at risk?" J of Autism Dev Disord. 32: 217-224.

Dawson, Michelle et al. "Learning in Autism." Excerpt from Learning and memory: A comprehensive reference: Cognitive Psychology. J.H. Byrne (Series Ed.) & H. Roediger (Vol. Ed.) 2008, Academic Press.

de Boysson-Bardies, Bénédicte. How Language Comes to Children: From Birth to Two Years. Bradford Books, 2001.

DeLoache, Judy S. et al. "Do Babies Learn From Baby Media?" Psychological Science 2010: 21: 1570-1574.

Desimone, Robert. "How the Brain Pays Attention." 2007 Forum for the Future of Higher Education; Cambridge, Massachusetts; excerpted from Forum Futures, 2007.

Dickerson Mayes, Susan & Susan L. Calhoun. "Impact of IQ, SES, gender, and race on autistic symptoms." Research in Autism Spectrum Disorders: 5 (2011) 749-757.

Dolcos, F. & G. McCarthy. "Brain Systems Mediating Cognitive Interference by Emotional Distraction." The Journal of Neuroscience. 2006; 26(7): 2072-2079.

Dolcos, F. et al. "Interaction Between the Amygdala and the Medial Temporal Lobe Memory System Predicts Better Memory for Emotional Events." Neuron. (2004) 42, 855-863.

Dolcos, F. et al. "Remembering One Year Later: Role of the Amygdala and the Medial Temporal Lobe Memory System During Retrieval of Emotional Memories." Proceedings of the National Academy of Sciences, USA. 2005; 102(7): 2626-2631.

Dumont-Mathieu, Thyde & Deborah Fein. "Screening for Autism in Young Children: The Modified Checklist for Autism in Toddlers (M-CHAT) and Other Measures." Mental Retardation and Developmental Disabilities. 11: 253-262 (2005).

Duncan, John et al. "Competitive brain activity in visual attention." Current Opinions in Neurobiology. 1997, 7:255-261.

Eigsti, Inge-Marie et al. "Language acquisition in autism spectrum disorders: A developmental review." Research in Autism Spectrum Disorders. 5 (2011) 681–691.

Fernald, Anne. "Four-Month-Old Infants Prefer to Listen to Motherese." Infant Behavior and Development 8, 181-195 (1985).

Ford Burac, Carolyn G. "Feral and Autistic Children: Integrating Disabled Children Who are Inept of Human Socialization & Development into Education and Society – A Literature Review." 2009; Lecture Notes EDF 6211 Foundations of Educational Psychology; University of South Florida.

Formby, David. "Maternal Recognition of Infant's Cry." Developmental Medicine & Child Neurology June 1967: Volume 9 Issue 3, pp 293-298.

Foudon, Nadège et al. "Language Acquisition in Autistic Children: A Longitudinal Study." CamLing. 2007: 72-79.

Frank Masur, Elise & Valerie Flynn. "Infant and mother-infant play and the presence of the television." Journal of Applied Developmental Psychology. 29 (2008) 76-83.

Frith, Chris. "A framework for studying the neural basis of attention." Neuropsychologia. 39 (2001): pp 1367–1371.

Greenspan, Stanley & Stuart Shanker. "The developmental pathways leading to pattern recognition, joint attention, language and cognition." New Ideas in Psychology. 25 (2007) 128-142.

Hammock, Elizabeth A.D. & Karry J. Young. "Oxytocin, vasopressin and pair bonding: implications for autism." Philosophical Transactions of the Royal Society B. (2006) B, 2187-2198.

Harlow, Harry F. & Stephen J. Suomi. "Social Recovery by Isolation-Reared Monkeys." Proceedings of the National Academy of Sciences USA Vol. 68, No. 7, pp. 1534-1538, July 1971.

Hoksbergen, Rene et al. "Post-Institutional Autistic Syndrome in Romanian Adoptees." Journal of Autism and Developmental Disorders. Vol. 35, No. 5. October 2005. Pp 615-623.

Hughes, John R. "Update on autism: A review of 1300 reports published in 2008." Epilepsy & Behavior. 16 (2009) 569-589.

Hunter, D. S. "Nicola: The use of sign language with a blind, autistic child." Child and Youth Care Forum 1983: 12(4); 321-336.

Kaland, Nils. "Social communication impairments in children and adolescents with Asperger syndrome: Slow response time and the impact of prompting." Research in Autism Spectrum Disorders. 5 (2011): pp 1129–1137.

Kana, Rajesh K. et al. "A systems level analysis of the mirror neuron hypothesis and imitation impairments in autism spectrum disorders." Neuroscience and Biobehavioral Reviews. 35 (2011) 894–902.

Kaplan, Peter S. et al. "Habituation, Sensitization, and Infants' Responses to Motherese Speech." Developmental Psychobiology. 28(1): 4S-57 (1995).

Kasari, Connie et al. "Affective Sharing in the Context of Joint Attention Interactions of Normal, Autistic, and Mentally Retarded Children." Journal of Autism and Developmental Disorders. 1990: Vol. 20, No. 1, pp 87-100.

Kidwell, Mardi & Don H. Zimmerman. "Joint attention as action." Journal of Pragmatics. 39 (2007): pp 592–611.

Kimura, D. Sex and Cognition. Cambridge, Mass.: MIT Press/Bradford Books, 1997.

LaBar, Kevin S. & Roberto Cabeza. "Cognitive neuroscience of emotional memory." Nature Reviews Neuroscience. (January 2006): 7, 54-64.

Langen, Marieke et al. "The neurobiology of repetitive behavior: ... and men." Neuroscience and Biobehavioral Review. (2010), doi: 10.1016, pp 1-10.

Lewis, Fiona M. et al. "Linguistic abilities in children with autism spectrum disorder." Research in Autism Spectrum Disorders. 1 (2007): pp 85–100.

Lillienthal, Nicole. "Autism, Blindness and Sign Language: A Case Study." 2003 FLASHA Convention, Presentation.

Linebarger, Deborah & Sarah Vaala. "Screen media and language development in infants and toddlers: An ecological perspective." Developmental Review 30 (2010): 176-202.

Liu, Yong et al. "Whole brain functional connectivity in the early blind." Brain. (2007) 130, pp 2085-2096.

Mahdhaoui, Ammar et al. "Computerized home video detection for motherese may help to study impaired interaction between infants who become infants and their parents." International Journal of Methods in Psychiatric Research. 20 (1): e6-e18 (2011).

Martin, François & Jennifer Farnum. "Animal-Assisted Therapy for Children With Pervasive Developmental Disorders." Western Journal of Nursing Research. 2002, 24(6), pp 657-670.

McDowell, Maxson J. "Is Autism Statistically Linked to Early Non-Maternal Child Care?" 2004 [Journal (On-line/Unpaginated)] (In Press).

Miles, Judith H. "Autism spectrum disorders – A genetics review." Genetics in Medicine. Vol. 13, No. 4. April 2011; pp 278-294.

Moore, Tirin. "The neurobiology of visual attention: finding sources." Current Opinion in Neurobiology. 2006, 16: pp 159–165.

Morales, Michael et al. "Following the Gaze and Development of Language in 6-Month-Olds." INFANT BEHAVIOR & DEVELOPMENT. 1998: 21 (2), pp. 373-377.

Morales, Michael et al. "Gaze following, temperament, and language development in 6-month-olds: A replication and extension." Infant Behavior & Development. 23 (2000): pp 231–236.

Morales, Michael et al. "Responding to Joint Attention Across the 6- Through 24-Month Age Period and Early Language Acquisition." Journal of Applied Developmental Psychology. 2000: 21(3), pp 283–298.

Munasib, Abdul & Samrat Bhattacharya. "Is the 'Idiot's Box' raising idiocy? Early and middle childhood television watching and child cognitive outcome." Economics of Education Review. 29 (2010) 873-883.

Mundy, Peter & Antoinette Gomes. "Individual Differences in Joint Attention Skill Development in the Second Year." INFANT BEHAVIOR & DEVELOPMENT. 1998: 21 (3), pp. 469-482.

Mundy, Peter & William Jarold. "Infant joint attention, neural networks and social cognition." Neural Networks. 23 (2010) 985-997.

Myers, Scott M. "Management of Children With Autism Spectrum Disorders." PEDIATRICS. Vol. 120, No. 5 November 2007. Pp 1162-1182.

Nelson, Charles A. & Monica Luciana (editors). Handbook of developmental cognitive neuroscience. Cambridge, Mass.: MIT Press, 2001.

Peterson, Candida & Siegal, Michael. "Insights into Theory of Mind from Deafness and Autism." Mind & Language. 2000:15 (1), pp 123-145

Pacherie, Elisabeth & Jerome Dokie. "From mirror neurons to joint actions." Cognitive Systems Research. 7 (2006) 101-112.

Paterson, Sarah J. et al. "Development of structure and function in the infant brain: Implications for cognition, language and social behaviour." Neuroscience and Behavioral Reviews. 30 (2006) 1087-1105

Pempek, T.A. et al. "The impact of infant directed videos on parent child interaction." Journal of Applied Developmental Psychology. (2011) 32, 10-19.

Pentland, Alex. "On the Collective Nature of Human Intelligence." Adaptive Behavior. 2007, 15: 189-197.

Pierce, Karen et al. "Detecting, Studying, and Treating Autism Early: The One-Year Well-Baby Check-Up Approach." The Journal of Pediatrics. September 2011. Vol. 159, Issue 3. Pp 458-465.e6.

Plauche Johnson, Chris et al. "Identification and Evaluation of Children with Autism Spectrum Disorders." PEDIATRICS. Vol. 120, No. 5 November 2007. Pp 1183-1211

Prezbindowski, Amy K. et al. "Joint Attention in Deaf and Hearing 22 Month-Old Children and Their Hearing Mothers." Journal of Applied Developmental Psychology. 1998: 19(3), pp 377-387.

Reddy, Vasudevi. "On being the object of attention: implications for self-other consciousness." TRENDS in Cognitive Sciences. September 2003. Vol. 7 No. 9. Pp 397-402.

Rizzolatti, Giacomo & Maddalena Fabbri-Destro. "The mirror system and its role in social cognition." Current Opinion in Neurobiology. 2008, 18:179–184.

Roelfsema, Martine T.; Hoekstra, Rosa A.; Allison, Carrie; Wheelwright, Sally; Brayne, Carol; Matthews, Fiona E. and Baron-Cohen, Simon." Are autism spectrum conditions more prevalent in an information technology region? A school-based study of three regions in the Netherlands." Journal of Autism and Developmental Disorders. 2011; in press.

Ronald A, Hoekstra RA. "Autism Spectrum Disorders and Autistic Traits: A Decade of New Twin Studies." American Journal of Medical

Rutter, Michael et al. "Early adolescent outcomes of institutionally deprived and non-deprived adoptees. III. Quasi-autism." Journal of Child Psychology and Psychiatry 48:12 (2007), pp 1200-1207.

Schultz, Robert T. "Developmental deficits in social perception in autism: the role of the amygdala and fusiform face area." International Journal of Developmental Neuroscience. 2005 Apr-May; 23(2-3): 125-41.

Smelser, Neil J. & Paul B. Baltes. International Encyclopedia of the Social & Behavioral Sciences. 2001. Elsevier Ltd.

Solomon, Olga. "What a Dog Can Do: Children with Autism and Therapy Dogs in Social Interaction." ETHOS. 2010: Vol. 38, Issue 1, pp. 143–166.

Stauder, J.E.A. et al. "The Extreme Male Brain theory and gender role behaviour in persons with an autism spectrum condition." Research in Autism Spectrum Disorders. 5 (2011) 1209-1214

Swing, Edward L. et al. "Television and Video Game Exposure and the Development of Attention Problems." Pediatrics 2010; 126; 214.

Syal, Supriya & Barbara L. Finlay. "Thinking outside the cortex: social motivation in the evolution and development of language." Developmental Science. 14:2 (2011), pp 417-430.

Tager-Flusberg, Helen. "Evaluating the Theory-of-Mind Hypothesis of Autism." Current Directions in Psychological Science. 2007. Vol. 16 No 6. Pp 311-315.

Tanguay, Peter E. et al. "A Dimensional Classification of Autism Spectrum Disorder by Social Communication Domains." Journal of the American Academy of Child & Adolescent Psychiatry. 1998, 37:3, pp 271-277.

Taylor Rivet, Teresa & Johnny L. Matson. "Review of gender differences in core symptomatology in autism spectrum disorders." Research in Autism Spectrum Disorders. 5 (2011) 957-976.

Thorpe, Karen. "Twin children's language development." Early Human Development. (2006) 82, pp 387-395.

Tomblin, J. Bruce. "Autism and autism risk in siblings of children with specific language impairment." International Journal of Language & Communication Disorders. 2003, Vol. 38, No. 3, 235–250.

Vandewater, Elizabeth A. et al. "When the Television Is Always On: Heavy Television Exposure and Young Children's Development." American Behavioral Scientist. 2005; 48: 562-577.

Vernes, Sonja C. et al. "Functional genetic analysis of mutations implicated in a human speech and language disorder." Human Molecular Genetics. 2006, Vol. 15, No. 21, pp 3154–3167.

Waldman, Michael; Sean Nicholson & Nodir Adilov. "Does Television Cause Autism?" December 2006. NBER Working Paper No. 12632.

Wartella, Ellen et al. "Babies, television and videos: How did we get here?" Developmental Review. 30 (2010) 116-127.

Zimmerman, Frederick J. et al. "Associations between Media Viewing and Language Development in Children Under Age 2 Years." The Journal of Pediatrics October 2007: 04. 071. Pp 364-368.

Zimmermann, Andrew W. (ed.) Autism: Current Theories and Evidence. October 2008, Springer-Verlag New York, LLC.